GOD'S GOT YOU COVERED

WHY BACK DOWN WHEN GOD IS BACKING YOU UP?

By

Edward N. Udeh

God's Got You Covered: © 2005 by
Edward N. Udeh

Published by:
Resurrection Power Outreach Ministries
P.O. Box 20228
Bloomington, MN 55420
(952) 881-2405

Unless otherwise noted, all scripture quotations are
from the King James or New International Versions of
the Bible.

Library of Congress Control Number: 2005902518
ISBN: 0-9760861-0-7

1st Edition 2005
Printed in the United States of America.

For worldwide distribution

WARNING!

Satan does not want you to read this book. He understands very well that if you do, the revelation and information you receive will empower you with the anointed spiritual tools you need to believe God for the breakthrough you desperately need and equip you to handle the everyday battles of life.

In addition, he does not want you to read this book because he understands that if you do, it will motivate and provoke a rise to a new level in your life. Furthermore, he knows that if you read through the pages of this book, it will challenge and stir up your faith to begin living a defeat-free life. Not only that, the Devil knows that if you read this book, it will show you how to put feet under your faith and stand your ground, even in the face of inevitable and seemingly insurmountable challenges.

He also knows that failure, defeat, and destruction come upon people's lives as a result of their lack of knowledge or ignorance of the purpose, plans, and promises of God for His children. The Lord said, *"My people are destroyed for lack of knowledge" (Hosea 4:6).*

Above all, Satan does not want you to know that **GOD'S GOT YOU COVERED** in every area of your life. This book will help you discover your rights, benefits, and privileges in God.

I strongly encourage you to take some time to read through the materials in this book because I believe that the revelation and information you will get out of it will position you to see the power of God working on your behalf.

INTRODUCTION

This book was born through revelations from the Word of God and my twenty-eight years of encounters and experiences with Him. The revelations given to me by the Spirit of God to share in this book have transformed and turned my life around. I trust that God will use it to turn your life around, as well.

The main purpose of the book is to teach you how to use the "power of persistent faith and determination" to obtain the breakthrough you desperately need even in the face of life's difficult challenges. This book also is intended to teach you how to use the "power of persistent faith and determination" to fight a spiritual warfare and overcome the battles of life, against all odds.

Therefore, get ready to move forward and higher to a new spiritual plane from where you are now. I believe with all my heart that the revelations in this book will arm you with new and powerful spiritual tools to help you begin to enjoy a defeat free life. In addition, one of my missions is to take you through many portions of God's words to show you how God used the "power of persistent faith and determination" to perform tremendous breakthroughs in the lives of ordinary people. These historical characters dared to not back down even in the face of what seemed to be immovable mountains and difficult challenges of life.

It is vital to point out that there is no defeat or surrender in God's vocabulary and neither must there be any in ours! I will share with you how you can use the Word, in conjunction with your faith, to help you overcome your challenges. It is only your faith in the word of God that makes you whole.

The Spirit of the living God has helped me

discover that the "master key" to a defeat-free life is the "power of persistent faith and determination." Indeed, I have discovered that all the issues, challenges, and battles of life can be overcome by appropriating the "power of persistent faith and determination." He reveals, through the pages of the Bible, how God turned the lives of ordinary men and women around. He did this even when their backs were against a wall. In another words, these ordinary men and women obtained tremendous victories in the face of probable defeat because they refused to back down. The Bible records,

> *And from the days of John the Baptist*
> *until now the kingdom of heaven*
> *suffereth violence, and the violent take*
> *it by force. (Mathew 11:12)*

This portion of the scripture and our every day experiences prove to us that life is a long journey and our days are spent in battles.

> *But thanks be to God, who gives us the*
> *victory through our Lord Jesus Christ.*
> *(1 Corinthians 15:57)*

We find in the word of God that He has already made provisions for us to enjoy victory in our every day battles of life. It is crucial to point out that God never promised us battle-free lives. But He assuredly guarantees us defeat-free lives.

It is also very important to point out that there is no victory without battle, no miracle without a mess, no breakthrough without going through trouble, no healing without disease or sickness to cure, and no over-coming without an obstacle.

Therefore, when the Bible says that God gives us

victory through Jesus Christ, it is incorrect to assume that our lives will be battle-free. Many people, especially new believers in Christ, wrongfully assume that as soon as they become Christians, they will begin to live battle-free lives. But that is not the case! I wish it were the case! In fact, the beginning of our walk and relationship with God, through our Lord and Savior Jesus Christ, is also the beginning of our life of battles with the Devil and his forces. No wonder the Apostle Paul exhorts us in one of his writings to,

> *Put on the whole of armour of God, that ye may be able to stand against the wiles of the devil; for we wrestle not against flesh and blood, but against principalities, against powers, against the rulers of darkness of this world, against spiritual wickedness in high places. (Ephesians 6:12-13)*

This book will show you how to appropriate the "power of persistent faith and determination" to fight for and receive what already belongs to you. I want to conclude this introduction by saying that wishing for your breakthrough will not get you the breakthrough you desperately need, but fighting for it, in God's way, will. King David said,

> *Blessed be the Lord my strength, which teacheth my hands to war, and my fingers to fight. (Psalm 144:1)*

There is no question about it, in the pages of the Bible we see how ordinary folk obtained tremendous victories when they appropriated the "power of persistent faith and determination" even in the face of very difficult and terrible situations. We will examine the lives of these men and women and find applications for our own lives.

> *Then Jesus told his disciples a parable to show them that they should always pray and not give up. He said: in a certain town there was a judge who neither feared God nor cared about men. And there was a widow in that town who kept coming to him with the plea, grant me justice against my adversary. For some time he refused. But finally he said to himself, even though I don't fear God or care about men, yet because this widow keeps bothering me, I will see that she gets justice, so that she won't eventually wear me out with her coming. And the Lord said, listen to what the unjust judge says. And will not God bring about justice for his chosen ones, who cry out to Him day and night? Will he keep putting them off? I tell you, He will see that they get justice, and quickly. However, when the Son of Man comes, will He find faith on the earth?*
> *(Luke 18:1-8)*

It is the sincere desire of my heart to help equip believers with the knowledge of what the Bible says about ordinary people, such as you and me, whose lives were turned around because they applied the principles of the "power of persistent faith and determination" and how this powerful principle helped them live defeat-free. It is also my earnest prayer that as you read through the pages of this book that your faith would grow mightily to believe God for the breakthrough you need today in Jesus' name.

DEDICATION

I dedicate this book to the Son of the Living God, Jesus Christ. He is the Lord and Savior of my life without whom I am nothing.

SPECIAL THANKS

I thank my Creator, God the Father, Son and Holy Ghost without whose inspiration this book could not have been written. My heartfelt thanks to my darling wife, Roselyn N. Udeh and my precious children: Christian, Godson, Faith, Gloria, Grace, Emmanuel, and Victoria for their immeasurable love, encouragement and support. I will ever be grateful to them. I also extend a heart full of thanks to my wonderful friends; Professor Larry Hackett, Evangelist Bridget Bazunu, Pastor Jerry Hauser and Dr. Jim Kaseman for their encouragement and contributions. A word of special thanks must go to Jerry Smith and Pastor Marcus Folarin for their encouragement and support.

I thank God for our church family from Resurrection Power Church International for their love and prayers. They are indeed vessels of honor unto God. Finally, I am thankful to beloved brothers and sisters in the Lord, pastor friends and colleagues too numerous to mention. May God's richest blessing rest on them always!

Table of Contents

Chapter 1

WHO IS THIS GOD THAT HAS YOU COVERED?

Philip said, Lord, show us the Father and that will be enough for us. Jesus answered: Don't you know me, Philip, even after I have been among you such a long time? Anyone who has seen me has seen the Father. How can you say, Show us the Father? Don't you believe that I am in the Father, and that the Father is in me? The words I say to you are not just my own. Rather, it is the Father, living in me, who is doing his work. Believe me when I say that I am in the Father and the Father is in me, or at least believe me on the evidence of the miracles themselves. (John 14:8-11)

My dear friend, I hope it does not surprise you to know that the precise question the Apostle Philip asked Jesus more than two thousand years ago, concerning whom God the Father is and how they could better know Him, is still being asked by many people today. The Bible tells us that, Philip said,

Lord, show us the Father and that will be enough for us. (John 14:8)

13

Like Philip, you may have such questions as, Who is this God the Father that "has got you covered" in every area of your life? How can you know Him more intimately? Why should you bother to know Him? In this chapter, I will, with the help of the Holy Spirit, deal concisely with these and other questions concerning whom God the Father is and how we can intimately know Him as our heavenly Father.

THE GOD OF ALL CREATION

In the beginning God created the heaven and earth. And the earth was without form, and void; and darkness was upon the face of the deep. And the Spirit of God moved upon the face of the waters. And God said, let there be light: and there was light. And God said, let the earth bring forth the living creature after his kind, cattle, and creeping thing, and beast of the earth after his kind: and it was so. And God made the beast of the earth after his kind, and cattle after their kind, and everything that creepeth upon the earth after his kind: and God saw that it was good. And God said let us make man in our own image, after our likeness: and let them have dominion over the fish of the sea, and over the fowl of the air, and over the cattle, and over all the earth, and over every creeping thing that creepeth upon the earth. So God created man in his own image, in the image of God created he him; male and female created he them. And God blessed them, and said unto them, Be fruitful, and multiply, and replenish the earth, and subdue it: and have dominion over the fish of the sea, and over the fowl of the air, and over every living thing that moveth upon the earth. (Genesis 1:1-3, 24-28)

According to this portion of the scripture, we learn that in the beginning God the Father created the heaven, earth, and all that is therein. If He created the heaven, earth, and everything in the beginning, then, God the Father existed before the beginning of creation. In other words, God is infinite. He has no beginning and no end. The Bible tells us that He is the everlasting God. He occupies the entire space both seen and unseen. The Bible further tells us that

God is a Spirit: and they that worship him must worship him in spirit and in truth. (John 4:24)

This means that in order for you to know this "God who has got you covered" in every area of your life, you must live in the spirit realm. Later in the chapter we will see how the sacrificial shed blood of Jesus Christ has made it possible for mortal mankind to live, walk, and fellowship with immortal God in the spirit while still in this earthly body. Additionally, the scripture records

For in him we live, and move, and have our being. (Acts 17:28)

This is a very powerful revelation that only the Holy Spirit of God can explain to mortal mankind. I trust that the Holy Spirit of God will enlighten your spiritual eyes of understanding so you can know God the

Father more intimately.

Based on these scriptures, we can firmly say that God is the Creator of heaven, earth, everything beneath the earth, and all that is therein. We learn that God also created Adam and Eve, the first persons of the human race and put them in a place perfectly designed by God Himself called the Garden of Eden. He gave them detailed instructions on how they should live there. The scripture tells us,

> *And the Lord God took the man, and put him into the Garden of Eden to dress it and to keep it. And the Lord God commanded the man, saying, Of every tree of the Garden thou mayest freely eat. But of the tree of the knowledge of good and evil, thou shall not eat of it: for in the day that thou eatest thereof thou shalt surely die. (Genesis 2:15-17)*

But things went wrong. Adam and Eve failed to observe the instructions God had given to them. They disobeyed His commandment and in so doing, sinned against Him. Oh! What a tragic and costly mistake that was! The scripture says

> *And when the woman saw that the tree was good for food, and that it was pleasant to the eyes, and a tree to be desired to make one wise, she took of the fruit of the tree thereof, and did eat, and gave also unto her husband with her; and he did eat. And the eyes of them both were opened, and they knew that they were naked; and they sewed fig leaves together, and made*

themselves aprons. And they heard the voice of the Lord God walking in the Garden in the cool of the day: and Adam and his wife hid themselves from the presence of the Lord God amongst the trees of the Garden. (Genesis 3:6-8)

As a result of their disobedience, their perfect relationship and fellowship with the holy and immortal God was broken. The honor, power, and authority that God had bestowed upon them were also lost. The scripture tells us that as a consequence of Adam and Eve's disobedience, God rendered judgment upon them and the Devil that deceived them. God cursed them!

Therefore the Lord God sent him forth from the Garden of Eden, to till the ground from whence he was taken. So he drove out the man; and placed at the east of the Garden of Eden cherubims, a flaming sword which turned every way, to keep the way of the tree of life. (Genesis 3:23-24).

When they sinned against God, one of the tragic and terrible consequences was that every person born of woman became a debtor for their sin and all the troubles that came with it. Because sin is the source of all the troubles in life, therefore, as a result of the sin of Adam and Eve, hell was opened as a punishment for the human race. Also, sickness, perilous times, diseases, death, sorrow, fearfulness, hatred, hardship, and all the consequences that came along with sin began to impact mankind.

LORD HELP ME TO GET MY LOST GLORY BACK

We were created in the very image and likeness of God to have dominion and oversee all the works of God's hands, as scripture clearly records. As consequences for the disobedience and sin of Adam and Eve, mankind lost the authority to be in charge of all the works of God's hands. The Bible tells us:

> What is man, that thou art mindful of him? and the son of man, that thou visitest him? For thou hast made him a little lower than the angels, and hast crowned him with glory and honor. Thou madest him to have dominion over the works of thy hands; thou hast put all things under his feet. All sheep and oxen, yea, and beasts of the field. The fowl of the air and the fish of the sea, and whatsoever passeth through the path of the seas. O LORD our Lord, how excellent is thy name in all the earth. (Psalm 8:4-9)

When it seemed like all hope was doomed and the human race was lost, the unmerited mercy and immeasurable love of God manifested.

THE GOD OF A SECOND CHANCE SENT THE SECOND ADAM

> For as by one man's [Adam] disobedience many were made sinners, so by the obedience of one [Jesus

18

Christ] shall many be made righteous.
(Romans 5:19)

Hallelujah! In the process of time God sent a second Adam, the Lord Jesus Christ, into the world to restore us to our original place of power, honor, and glory. After thousands of years of broken union between a holy and immortal God and sinful mortal mankind, the Lord Jesus Christ came into the world to pay the ultimate price for sin. God the Father laid the sins and the wages of sins of the first Adam upon the head of the second Adam, the Lord Jesus Christ. He shed His precious blood for the sin of the whole world and in so doing restored the broken relationship and fellowship between God and mankind. The Bible records:

> *All we like sheep have gone astray; we have turned every man to his own way; and the Lord hath laid upon him the iniquity of us all. (Isaiah 53:6)*
> *The wages of sin is death, but the gift of God is eternal life through Jesus Christ. (Romans 6:23)*

Biblically, blood sacrifice with a spotless lamb was very crucial to the redemption process. We find evidence, throughout the pages of the Bible, to support the fact that in order for redemption from sin to occur and forgiveness to be received, a spotless lamb must be sacrificed. God the Father, the Creator of all things, out of His immeasurable mercy and love towards mankind, provided His spotless Lamb as a substitution for all of our sins. Through the sacrificial shed blood of the Lord Jesus Christ, the acceptable Lamb of God, all those who believe in Him are redeemed, forgiven, justified, and reconciled to God.

19

Praise God!

> *Forasmuch as ye know that ye were not redeemed with corruptible things, as silver and gold, from your vain conversation received by tradition from your fathers. But with the precious blood of Christ, as of a lamb without blemish and without spot.*
> *(1 Peter 1:18-19)*
> *The next day John seeth Jesus coming unto him, and saith, Behold the Lamb of God which taketh away the sin of the world. (John 1:29)*
> *And almost all things are by law purged with blood; for without shedding of blood is no remission. (Hebrews 9:22)*
> *For God commended his love toward us, in that while we were yet sinners, Christ died for us. (Romans 5:8).*
> *For God so loved the world that He gave His only begotten Son that whosoever believeth in Him should not perish but have everlasting life. For God sent not His Son into the world to condemn the world; but that the world through Him might be saved. He that believeth on Him is not condemned: but He that believeth not is condemned already because he hath not believed in the name of the only begotten Son of God. (John 3:16-18).*

My dear friend, our God is a God of the second chance. We lost everything God had bestowed upon us when the first Adam sinned, but through the second Adam we are restored. You may have blown many God given opportunities in your life, as I have done myself several times. However, I have good news for you. God always wants to give you another chance regardless of what you may have done previously. He is a God of restoration, and He wants to restore to you all the lost opportunities that you may have blown. Praise the Lord! Let us dig deeper into the Bible to know more about this God!

GOD THE FATHER REVEALED
IN JESUS CHRIST

The Lord Jesus Christ is the "image of the invisible God" (Colossians 1:15). The Bible also declares,

> *God, who at sundry times and in divers manners spake in time past unto the fathers by the prophets, hath in these last days spoken unto us by his Son, whom he hath appointed heir of all things, by whom also he made the worlds. (Hebrews 1:1-2)*
> *No man has ever seen God, but God the One and Only, who is at the Father's side, has made him known. (John 1:18)*
> *Thomas said to him, Lord, we don't know where you are going, so how can we know the way? Jesus answered, I am the way, and the truth, and the life. No one comes to the Father except through me. If you really knew me, you would know my Father as well. From now on, you do know him, and have seen him. (John 14:5-7).*
> *I and the Father are one. (John 10:30)*

In these portions of the word of God, we find the only way to intimately know this "God who has you covered" in all the areas of your life, is to know the Lord Jesus Christ. Since Jesus Christ is the express image of God the Father, the only sure way you can fully and intimately know who God the Father is, is to have a full grasp and knowledge of whom Jesus Christ is. This is because God the Father revealed Himself to mankind through His only Son, the Lord Jesus Christ. Jesus said, *"I and the Father are one."*

There is overwhelming evidence in the Bible supporting the fact that the Lord Jesus Christ, the only Son of God, and God the Father are one. Let us look closely at a few portions of the scripture for our exhortation. This is very important because if you get the revelation of whom Jesus Christ is, then, you automatically know who God the Father is also. My dear friend, what a blessing will come upon your life when you grasp this revelation! In the Apostle John's gospel we find the following:

> *In the beginning was the Word, and the Word was with God, and the Word was God. The same was in the beginning with God. All things were made by him; and without him was not any thing made that was made. (John 1:1-3).*
> *For there are three that bear record in heaven, the Father, the Word,[Jesus Christ] and the Holy Ghost: and these three are one. (1 John 5:7)*

Since no one can fully know who God the Father is, without full knowledge of who Jesus Christ is, there are three biblically stipulated steps that must be taken in order for you to fully and intimately know the Lord Jesus Christ.

HAVE A PERSONAL RELATIONSHIP
AND A CLOSE WALK WITH
JESUS CHRIST

First, you must have a personal relationship with the Lord. For instance, is it realistic for someone to have an intimate relationship with another person without constantly spending quality time with that person? The answer is emphatically no. So, in order for you to intimately know God the Father "who has you covered" in all the areas of your life, you must establish a personal relationship with the Lord Jesus Christ and have a close walk with Him.

To have a personal relationship with the Lord and be a true follower of the Lord means that

- First, we must acknowledge our sins and confess them to the Lord and ask for forgiveness.
- Second, we must receive the Lord into our hearts as our personal Lord and Savior.
- Third, we must commit wholeheartedly to follow the Lord as long as we live, come what may.
- Fourth, we must make a public identification, declaration, and confession of His lordship over our lives.

You must accept God's redemptive plan for mankind. This plan for mankind is wrapped up in Jesus Christ, the only begotten Son of God. The plan is that, through the sacrificial blood of Jesus Christ, all the sins of mankind are forgiven. This means that you must acknowledge your sins before God because the Bible says, *For all have sinned, and come short of the glory of God." (Romans 3:23),* and

23

humbly ask God's forgiveness of all of your sins. You then invite Jesus Christ into your heart as Lord and Savior of your life. In other words, you must be "born again."

Let me explain more in detail with an example from the Bible to help illustrate our discussion. The Bible tells us:

> *There was a man of the Pharisees, named, Nicodemus, a ruler of the Jews. The same came to Jesus by night, and said unto him, Rabbi, we know that thou art a teacher came from God: for no man can do these miracles that thou dost, except God be with him. Jesus answered and said unto him, verily, verily, I say unto thee, except a man be born again, he cannot see the Kingdom of God, Nicodemus saith unto him, how can a man be born again when he is old? Can he enter the second time unto his mother's womb, and be born? Jesus answered, verily, verily, I say unto thee, except a man be born of water and of the Spirit, he cannot enter into the Kingdom of God. That which is born of the flesh is flesh; and that which is born of the Spirit is of the Spirit. Marvel not that I say unto thee, ye must be born again. (John 3:1-7)*

As we can see from the above scripture, Nicodemus was a very religious man; learned, and highly respected as a teacher of the law. But he had no personal relationship with God. My dear friend, there is wide difference between a religious relationship and a personal relationship with God. A person with a religious relationship strives to keep the rules, creeds or stipulated sets of laws, the "dos and don'ts" to be precise! But a person that has a personal relationship with God is one that believes and accepts the forgiveness for sin that comes only through the blood of Jesus Christ. He is one that depends on the unmerited grace of God and has no confidence in the works of his hands.

Getting back to the encounter between Nicodemus and the Lord, when he saw the miracles the Lord was performing among the people, he decided to meet with him secretly at night. He wanted to ask the Lord what he must do to inherit the Kingdom of God. The Lord commanded that he "must be born again" otherwise he had no part in the Kingdom of God. The Bible tells us that Nicodemus accepted the command of the Lord and became a secret disciple for fear of the Jews. Later, after the Lord was crucified, it was Nicodemus and Joseph that took good care of his body and prepared it for burial.

> *And after this Joseph of Arimathaea, being a disciple of Jesus, but secretly for the fear of the Jews, besought Pilate that he might take away the body of Jesus: Pilate gave him leave. He came therefore, and took the body of Jesus. And there came also Nicodemus, which at first came to Jesus by night, and brought a mixture of myrrh and aloes, about a hundred pound weight. Then took they the body of Jesus, and wound it in linen clothes with the spices, as the manner of the Jews is to bury. (John 19:38-40)*

As can be seen, from these portions of the

scripture, Nicodemus became a "born again" disciple and follower of the Lord Jesus Christ after he had an encounter with Him. Although, he was a secret disciple, for the fear of the Jews, he had a personal relationship and a close walk with God. In fact, he was delivered from the bondage of religion. In the same way, you must have an encounter with the Lord, and He will do for you what He did for Nicodemus. You must take a step of faith toward the Lord and He will never turn you away! Nicodemus' was changed for the best because he accepted the redemptive plan of God. If you do the same as Nicodemus did, I assure you a new life will begin for you.

Just as the Lord commanded Nicodemus, more than two thousand years ago, He is commanding all mankind that they too must be "born again." This is the redemptive plan of God for the human race. Therefore, in order to know God the Father "Who has got you covered", you must accept the redemptive plan of God the Father, by acknowledging your sin and receiving the Lord Jesus Christ into your heart as the Savior of your life.

> *If we say that we have no sin, we deceive ourselves, and the truth is not in us. If we confess our sins, he is faithful and just to forgive our sins, and to cleanse us from all unrighteousness. If we say that we have not sinned, we make him a liar, and his word is not in us. (1 John 1:8-10)*
> *Then will I sprinkle clean water [the word of God] upon you, and ye shall be clean: from all your filthiness, and from all your idols, will I cleanse you. And a new heart also will I give you, and a*

*new spirit will I put within you: and I will
take away the stony heart out of your
flesh; and I will give you a heart of flesh.
And I will put my spirit within you, and
cause you to walk in my statutes. And
ye shall keep my judgments, and do
them.*
(Ezekiel 36:25-27)

After you confess your sins to God and ask Him to
forgive your sins and receive the Lord Jesus Christ
as the Lord and Savior of your life, He will keep his
promise to abundantly forgive you all of your sins.
Then, God the Father will empower you to become
His child.

*But as many as received Him [Jesus
Christ] to them gave he the power to
become the sons of God, even to them
that believe on His name. (John 1:12)*

TELL OTHERS OF YOUR
NEW LIFE WITH JESUS CHRIST

Second, you must tell others of your new life with
the Lord Jesus Christ. This is a very crucial step
because, throughout the New Testament, every one
the Lord called he called publicly and openly. You
must confess the Lord Jesus Christ before others to
make a public declaration of your new walk and
relationship with God the Father through His dear
Son.

*Hereby know ye the Spirit of God: every
spirit that confesseth that Jesus Christ
is come in the flesh is of God.
(1John 4:2)*

27

That if thou shall confess with thy mouth the Lord Jesus, and shall believe in thine heart that God hath raised him from the dead, thou shall be saved. For with the heart man believeth unto righteousness; and with the mouth confession is made unto salvation. (Romans 10:9-10).
Whosoever therefore shall confess me before men, him will I confess before my Father which is in heaven. But whosoever shall deny me before men, him will I also deny before my Father which is in heaven. (Matthew 10:32-33).

FOLLOW HIM DAILY

He said to them all, if any man will come after me, let him deny himself, and take up his cross daily, and follow me. (Luke 9:23)

Third, in order to maintain your walk and relationship with the Lord Jesus Christ, you must follow Him daily, not when you feel like it. Child of God, as you know very well, following the Lord is not a matter of convenience but of commitment. There is a great difference! You must commit to follow the Lord, come what may, all the days of your life and follow Him daily not seasonally. There are many people who attend their places of worship three times yearly, namely Christmas Day, New Year's Day, and Easter Day services. These kinds of worshippers are the seasonal Christians. The Lord's command is that we take up our cross and follow Him daily. If you take these biblically stipulated steps described above, you are now "born again" and a member of the family of

God through the Lord Jesus Christ.

Now that you have begin a personal walk and relationship with the Lord Jesus Christ, "This God that has got you covered" in all the areas of your life is now revealed to you. Since you cannot know God the Father except through His only Son, Jesus Christ, by knowing Jesus Christ you now know God the Father.

YOU ARE NOW A BLOOD BOUGHT CHILD OF GOD

What? Know ye not that your body is the temple of the Holy Ghost which is in you, which ye have of God,, and ye not your own? For ye are bought with a price: therefore glorify God in your body, and in your spirit, which are God's(1 Corinthians 6:19-20)

When you take the steps discussed above, you become a child of the living God and a full citizen of the Kingdom of God. The Bible says,

But when the fullness of time was come, God sent his Son, made of a woman, made under the law to redeem them that were under the law, that we might receive the adoption of sons. And because you are sons, God hath sent the Spirit of his Son in your hearts, crying. Abba, Father. Wherefore thou art no more servant, but a son; and if a son, then an heir of God through Christ. (Galatians 4:3-7)

As a result of your new walk and relationship with

29

God the Father you are a child of God covered under the Blood covenant of God. Who is this God that has got you covered? He is Almighty God, the Creator of all things and the Father of our Lord and Savior Jesus Christ.

When you accept Jesus Christ as Savior and Lord of your life, God the Father then becomes your own heavenly Father. Everything He owns becomes your inheritance from that day forward. He is obligated and responsible for covering all the areas of your life. How about that? Isn't God good? He is!

Now that you are a member of the household of God, you cannot be fully complete and experience the goodness and wonder working power of God without knowledge of the Holy Spirit wanting to fill your life with Himself. In the time in which we live, it is the person of the Holy Spirit that reveals the fullness of the Lord Jesus Christ to us, after we are "born again." God the Father promised to put His Spirit into our lives to empower and enable us to be all that He has called us to be. So, it is your right and not a privilege to ask God for the full control of His mighty Holy Spirit in every area of your life. It is the person of the Holy Spirit who lives in us to glorify the Lord Jesus Christ. The word says:

> *Then will I sprinkle clean water [the word of God] upon you, and ye shall be clean: from all your filthiness, and from all your idol, will I cleanse you. And a new heart also will I give you, and a new spirit will I put within you: and I will take away the stony out of your flesh; and I will give a heart of flesh. And I will put my spirit within you, and cause you to walk in my statutes. And ye shall keep my judgments, and do them. (Ezekiel 36:26-27)*

Therefore, boldly and confidently ask God for the Holy Spirit and He will bless you with His Spirit, even right at this moment. The Lord said:

> *And I say unto you, Ask, and it shall be given you; seek, and ye shall find; knock, and it shall be opened unto you. For every one that asketh receiveth; and he that seeketh findeth; and to him that knocketh it shall be opened. If a son shall ask bread of any of you that is a father, will he give him a stone? Or if he ask for a fish, will he for a fish give him serpent? Or if he shall ask for an egg, will he offer him a scorpion? If ye then, being evil, know how to give good gifts unto your children: how much more shall your heavenly Father give the Holy Ghost to them that ask him.*
> *(Luke 11:9-13)*

Now that you know this "God that has got you covered" in all the areas of your life, the moment is come and the stage is set for you to discover your rights, privileges, and benefits as a blood-bought child of God.

Chapter 2

HE HAS GOT IT MADE FOR YOU

I am come that they might have life, and that they might have it more abundantly. (John 10:10)

In chapter one, we saw that the main purpose God the Father sent the second Adam, the Lord Jesus Christ, into the world was to pay the ultimate price for the sins of the whole world. Through His sacrificial shed blood on the Cross of Calvary, all who believe on His name might be forgiven, justified, sanctified, and restored to their original place of honor, power, and glory. Additionally, He came to reconcile us with God. The Lord also came so that those who believe on Him might have life and have it more abundantly.

My dear friend, the Lord came for your wholeness in every area of your life. God the Father, through the Lord Jesus Christ, has got it made for you! It is a done deal! Everything you need in life today, tomorrow, or in the future is in Jesus Christ. If you accept Him as the Lord and Savior of your life, you have access to everything that God the Father owns.

WHATEVER YOU NEED IS IN JESUS CHRIST

If you make a place in your life to be a dwelling place for Him to reside, you become a recipient of all that heaven has to offer. Our Lord Jesus Christ is the *"image of the invisible God." (Colossians 1:15)* Therefore, if you have the Lord Jesus Christ, you also have God the Father on your side. HE HAS GOT IT MADE FOR YOU!

Always remember that,

- He is your Strong Tower   Proverbs 18:10
- He is your Keeper   Psalm 121:5
- He is your Mediator   1 Timothy 2:5
- He is your Servant   Matthew 12:18
- He is your Healer   Isaiah 53:5
- He is your Watchman   Psalm 125:2
- He is your Strength   Nehemiah 10:8
- He is your Deliverer   Joel 2:32
- He is your Provider   Philippians 4:19
- He is your Good Shepherd   John 10:11
- He is your Helper   Psalm 124:8
- He is your Prince of Peace   John 16:33
- He is your Righteousness   Isaiah 54:17
- He is your Light   John 8:12
- He is your Bread of Life   John 6:35
- He is your Advocate   1 John 2:1
- He is your High Priest   Hebrew 6:20
- He is your Alpha and Omega   Revelation 22:13
- He is your Teacher   John 3:2
- He is your True Vine   John 15:1
- He is your Everlasting God   Isaiah 9:6
- He is your Messiah   Daniel 9:25

- He is your Emmanuel — Matthew 1:23
- He is your King of kings — 1 Timothy 6:15
- He is your Holy One — Mark 1:24
- He is your Lord of Lords — 1 Timothy 6:15
- He is your Bright Morning Star — Revelation 22:16
- He is your Way, Truth, & Life — John 14:6
- He is your I AM — Luke 8:58
- He is your Wonderful Counselor — Isaiah 9:6
- He is your Rock — 1 Corinthians 10:4
- He is your Head of the Church — Ephesians 5:23
- He is your DaySpring — Luke 1:78
- He is your Prophet — Matthew 21:11
- He is your Savior — John 4:42
- He is your Resurrection & Life — John 11:25
- He is your Redeemer — Job 19:25
- He is your Word of God — John 1:1
- He is your Anchor — Hebrew 6:19
- He is your Lion of the Tribe of Judah — Revelation 5:5
- He is your Carpenter — Mark 6:3
- He is your Chief Corner Stone — Ephesians 2:20
- He is your Author & Finisher of our Faith — Hebrews 12:2
- He is your Faithful & True Witness — Revelation 3:14
- He is your Living Water — John 4:10
- He is your Rose of Sharon — Songs of Solomon 2:1

- He is your Judge   Acts 10:42
- He is your Almighty   Revelation 1:8
- He is your Master   Mathew 8:19
- He is your Beginning
  & End   Revelation 22:13
- He is your Being   Acts 17:28
- He is your Bridegroom   Matthew 9:15
- He is your First & Last   Revelation 22:13
- He is your Jesus Christ   Hebrews 13:8
- He is your Amen   Revelation 3:14

Child of God, everything you need today or will ever need in life has already been paid for, packaged, and sealed, and is waiting for your taking. All you need to do is arise and possess your inheritance in Jesus Christ. The scriptures above are provided to help challenge and propel your faith to new heights so you can prayerfully believe God for the breakthrough you desperately need today. Therefore, I challenge you to arise and receive by faith those things that are rightfully yours, in Jesus' name.

Chapter 3

YOUR NAME IS IN HIS "WILL"

Neither by the blood of goats and calves, but by his blood he entered in once into the holy place, having obtained eternal redemption for us. For if the blood of bulls and of goats, and the ashes of an heifer sprinkling the unclean, sanctifieth to the purifying of the flesh. How much more shall the blood of Christ, who through the eternal Spirit offered himself without spot to God, purge your conscience from dead works to serve the living God. And for this cause he is the mediator of the new testament, that by means of death, for the redemption of the transgressions that were under the first testament, they which are called night receive the promise of eternal inheritance. For where a testament is, there must also of a necessity be the death of the testator. For a testament is of force after men are dead: otherwise it is of no strength at all while the testator liveth. Whereupon neither the first testament

was dedicated without blood.
(Hebrews 9:12-18)

Several years ago, I had automobile insurance coverage with All State Insurance Company. One of the privileges in my policy was a "free towing" benefit should my vehicle break down. Because I did not read thoroughly the contents in the policy I did not know that I had this benefit. On numerous occasions, I paid out of my pocket to tow my vehicle to the garage for repairs. Sadly enough, I did this for several years.

One day, a friend who had pitifully observed how much trouble my vehicle was giving me suggested that I call my agent and ask him to add a "free towing" clause to my policy. Surprisingly, when I called my agent, he told me that I already had "free towing." I was shocked and ashamed to hear this because I had put my family through some pain and hardship for something that was already mine. My loss was as a result of my lack of knowledge or ignorance of privileges and benefits in my insurance policy.

In the same way, many children of God languish in a great deal of pain, suffering, and hardship because of their lack of knowledge or ignorance of purposes, plans, and promises of God for their lives. Many children of God go through a lot of trouble because the Devil does not want them to know that God has already got them insured and covered through the blood of Jesus Christ. In my ordeal, should I have blamed the All State Insurance Company for my failure to find out what were my rightful privileges and benefits? The answer is emphatically no. Neither should any child of God blame Him for their ignorance or failure to take time to find out about God's insurance policy, His promises, and their benefits as blood-bought children of God.

In one of King David's writings, he said,

> *Bless the Lord, O my soul: and all that is within me, bless his holy name. Bless the Lord, O my soul, and forget not all his benefits: Who forgiveth all thine iniquities; who healeth all thine diseases; Who redeemeth thy life from destruction; who crowneth thee with lovingkindness and tender mercies; Who satisfieth thy mouth with good things; so that thy youth be renewed like the eagle's. (Psalm 103:1-5)*

As we see in the above portion of scripture, great King David instructed his soul not to forget all the benefits that were rightfully his as a child of God. King David must have read thoroughly the contents of the laws of God and discovered all the benefits that he had as a child of God. In fact, he knew that healing, forgiveness, mercies, satisfaction, and strength were some of God's benefits that belonged to him.

Child of God, it is a fact, you can never have what you do not know is rightfully yours. In this chapter, with the help of the Holy Spirit, you will discover that as a blood-bought child of God, "your name is in the "will"" as a result of the death of the Jesus Christ.

We find from our opening scriptures in the book of Hebrews that in the Old Testament it was a customary practice, before any covenant or "will" was entered, that there was a blood sacrifice to make it forceful and legal. In the same way, the Lord Jesus Christ, the spotless Lamb of God offered Himself as a sacrificial Lamb to enter into a "will" or covenant with God the Father on behalf of all who believe on His name. Through His name they can have access to all the blessings of God. If you are a believer on the name of Jesus Christ, your name is in the "will" and there are benefits awaiting for you that you may have not discovered. Let us go into the word of God to help you discover those benefits.

GOD'S GOT YOU COVERED UNDER THE NEW COVENANT

> *And it shall come to pass, that whosoever shall call on the name of the Lord shall be delivered. (Joel 2:32)*
> *The name of the Lord is a strong tower: the righteous runneth into it, and is safe. (Proverbs 18:10)*

There are seven redemptive covenant names of the Lord Jesus Christ covering the children of God in all areas of their lives. Now that you are a member of God's household you are under the new covenant. These are blood-bought redemptive covenants that God the Father made through the redemptive names of Jesus Christ for all who believe in the sacrifice of the Lord Jesus Christ. These names do not indicate privileges but rights for every blood-washed child of God. Therefore everything that you need or will ever need in life is already covered under the covenant names of the Lord.

Let us take a closer look at these seven redemptive covenant names. I believe it will stir your faith to believe and trust God for the breakthrough you desperately need today. First, the Bible tells us:

> *Christ hath redeemed us from the curse of the law, being made a curse for us: for it is written, cursed is every one that*

hangeth on a tree. That the blessing of Abraham might come on the Gentile through Jesus Christ: that we might receive the promise of the Spirit through faith. (Galatians 3:13-14)

The blood of the Lord Jesus Christ has redeemed us from every curse of the law. In order for us to be truly grateful and appreciate what the Lord's precious blood has already redeemed us from, we need to know how we are impacted by the curses of the law.

In Deuteronomy chapter twenty-eight, beginning from verse fifteen through verse sixty-eight, we find an extensive list of all the curses of the law from which the blood of the Lord Jesus Christ redeems us. We find that the curses of the law include sicknesses, sin, diseases, poverty, pain, terror, and bondage just to mention a few. All those who accept the Jesus Christ into their hearts as Lord and personal Savior, are redeemed from every one of these curses. This does not mean we are no longer harassed by the devil but that we are no longer held captive under the curses of the law. Praise the Lord for we are redeemed!

JEHOVAH TSIDKENU: THE LORD OUR RIGHTEOUSNESS

He is our righteousness! One blessing the new covenant redemptive blood of Jesus Christ has fetched for us is found in His redemptive name. He is our Jehovah Tsidkenu: The Lord our righteousness.

For Christ is the end of the law for righteousness to every one that believeth. (Romans 10:4)
Therefore as by the offence one [Adam

41

and Eve] judgment came upon all men to condemnation; even so by the righteousness of one [Jesus Christ] the free gift came upon all men unto justification of life. For as by one man's disobedience [Adam and Eve] many were made sinners, so by the obedience of one [Jesus Christ] shall many be made righteous.
(Romans 5:18-19)

One completed work on the Cross of Calvary was the redemption of our lives from the bondage of sinful and unrighteous living. The sacrificial blood of Jesus Christ was shed to redeem us from sin and through our faith in the Lord Jesus Christ we receive the righteousness of God that came upon us by grace and not of our works. As the scripture says, that *"by the offence of one man, Adam, every person that was born of woman was made a sinner, even so through the righteousness of one man, Jesus Christ, every one that believes can be made right with God."*

The work of righteousness has already been completed on the Cross of Calvary. It is a done deal! It is not earned by our good works or deeds; but by our faith in the sacrificial blood of the only begotten Son of God. The Bible tells us:

> *But as many as received him [Jesus Christ] to them gave he power to become the sons of God even to them that believe on his name. (John 1:12)*

When you are "born again" having accepted and received Jesus Christ into your heart, God the Father will then put His Son's righteousness into you and establish His covenant relationship with you.

Therefore you can gladly and boldly declare that "God has got you covered" through the blood of Jesus Christ and joyfully shout, "I have the righteousness of God!" In case the accuser of the brethren, the Devil and his forces, are bothering you with guilt and condemnation for your past sins and faults, all you need to do is call on the mighty name of the Lord, and run to Him and He will deliver and save you. He has promised to deliver and keep you safe from your enemies if you call on His name and run to Him.

JEHOVAH SHAMMAR: THE LORD IS PRESENT

Second, "God has got you covered" in the areas of safety and security of your life. He is our Jehovah Shammar.

> *God is our refuge and strength, a very present help in trouble. (Psalm 46:1)*
> *Fear thou not, for I am with thee: be not dismayed; for I am thy God: I will strength thee; yea, I will help thee; yea, I will uphold thee with the right hand of my righteousness. (Isaiah 41:10)*
> *And, lo, I am with you alway even unto end of the world, Amen.*
> *(Matthew 28:20)*

The second redemptive covenant name of the Lord is Jehovah Shammar, "The Lord is present." The moment we accept and receive the Lord into our heart, He promised to walk and be with us always even to the end of the world. As we journey in life, the most important thing we need is the presence of the Lord being with us wherever we go.

Yea, though I walk through the valley of
the shadow of death, I will fear no evil:
for thou art with me. (Psalms 23:4)

As a result of His shed blood all those who believe in His name have the mighty presence of the living God with them all the time. When we come into the family of God, by accepting Jesus Christ as Lord and Savior of our lives, we automatically become a temple in which God will dwell.

JEHOVAH SHOLOM: THE LORD OUR PEACE

Third, "God has got you covered," with the Peace of God! He is our Jehovah Sholom. Before the Lord Jesus Christ departed from the world, after His crucifixion and resurrection from the grave, He met with His disciples and exhorted them with these words:

Peace I leave with you, my peace I give
unto you: not as the world giveth, give I
unto you, let not your heart be troubled,
neither let it be afraid. (John 14:27)

It is the perfect "will" of God that His children live in peace and safety. The precious blood of the Lord Jesus Christ paid for our "peace of mind" all the days of our lives. We don't have to work for it all we need to do is receive the peace that He purchased for us. Before He was crucified, He promised His peace to all who would believe in His name. The peace of mind that you need resides inside Jesus Christ and when you accept and receive Him into your life, that peace of mind automatically comes with it. I understand that sometimes we are confronted with

44

many issues of life that may hamper with our peace and joy. But through it all you should always remember to call on His name for safety and deliverance. The Bible tells us:

> *For the Kingdom of God is not meat and drink; but righteousness, and peace, and joy in the Holy Ghost. (Romans 14:17).*

JEHOVAH EL-SHADAI: THE ONE THAT IS SUFFICIENT

Fourth, He is also our Jehovah El-Shadai. Everything that we need in life, today and may ever need, is already ours because the Lord Jesus Christ lives in us. We are complete in Him! He is the Lord that is more than enough! He is more than enough when you need financial blessing, healing, guidance, protection, deliverance, and prosperity. He is more than enough regardless of what your needs may be. Praise the Lord! He is able *"To do exceeding, abundantly above all that we ask or think." (Ephesians 3:20).* The Bible also tells us:

> *O taste and see that the Lord is good: blessed is the man that trusteth in him. O fear the Lord, ye his saints: for there is no want to them that fear him. The young lions do lack, and suffer hunger: but they that seek the Lord shall not want any good thing. (Psalm 34:8-10)*

Child of God, whatever your needs, whatever circumstances you may be faced with right now, our "God of more than enough," is able to fix and handle all the issues of life for you. Why not call on His name and run to it today? He has promised to deliver and save you when you do. Remember what the scriptures says,

> *Behold, I am the Lord, the God of all flesh: is any thing too hard for me? (Jeremiah 32:27)*
> *What shall we then say to these things? If God be for us, who can be against us? He that spared not his own Son, but delivered him up for us all, how shall he not with him also free give us all things? (Romans 8:31-32)*
> *I am the good shepherd: the good shepherd giveth His life for the sheep. (John 10:11).*
> *The Lord is my shepherd; I shall not want. (Psalm 23:1)*

JEHOVAH RAPHA: THE LORD OUR HEALER

Fifth, God the Father through the blood of Jesus has got you covered in the area of your health. He is our Jehovah Rapha, the Lord our healer.

Divine health is your right and not a privilege, as a child of God. As a result of your walk and relationship with God through the Lord Jesus Christ, you become the recipient of the covenant blessings of God. The Bible declares,

> *But he was wounded for our transgressions, he was bruised for our iniquities: the chastisement of our peace was upon him: and with his stripes we are healed. (Isaiah 53:5)*
> *And when Jesus was come into Peter's*

46

house, he saw his wife's mother laid, and sick of a fever. And he touched her hand, and the fever left her: and she arose, and ministered unto them. When the even was come, they brought unto him many that were possessed with Devils: and he cast out the spirits with his word, and healed all that were sick. That it might be fulfilled which was spoken by Esaias [Isaiah] the prophet, saying, himself took our infirmities and bear our sicknesses. (Matthew 8:14-17) Who his own self bare our sins in his own body on the tree, that we being, dead to sins, should live unto righteousness: by whose stripes ye were healed.
(1 Peter 2:24)

These portions of scripture certainly guarantee that through the sacrifice of the Lord Jesus Christ every one that believes in Him has been redeemed from the curses of the law including sicknesses and diseases. You may be afflicted with sickness and disease in your body right at this moment, I want to encourage you to put your faith to work and call on the name of the Lord, right now. Run to Him! He will save and deliver you. There is no question about it, the only way you can see the glory and power of God manifested in your life is to obey and act upon His word.

JEHOVAH NISI: THE LORD OUR VICTOR

Sixth, God the Father has got us covered through the precious blood of His Son and guarantees us victory and a defeat free-life. He is our Jehovah Nisi, the Lord our Victor.

> *But thanks be to God, which giveth us the victory through our Lord Jesus Christ. (1Corinthians 15:58)*
> *For whatsoever is born of God overcometh the world: and this is the victory that overcometh the world, even our faith. Who is he that overcometh the world, but he that believeth that Jesus is the Son of God. (1John 4-5)*

My dear friend, we have victory through the blood of Jesus Christ our Lord. So, regardless of the challenges you may face today, you are already a winner and you are emerging with your head lifted high in victory. Therefore stand strong in the Lord because

> *He who keeps you will never be asleep nor slumber. (Psalm 121:3)*

JEHOVAH JIRAH: THE LORD OUR PROVIDER

Finally, the seventh covenant blessing we have in Christ Jesus is that God the Father has assuredly guaranteed to be the source of our supply in every need that we have. He is our Jehovah Jirah, the Lord our provider.

> *The Lord is my shepherd and I shall not want. (Psalm 23:1)*
> *O taste and see that the Lord is good: blessed is the man that trusteth in him. O fear the Lord, ye his saints: for there is no want to them that fear him. The*

young lions do lack, and suffer hunger:
but they that seek the Lord shall not
want any good thing. (Psalm 34:8-10)
I have been young and now am old; yet
I have not seen the righteous forsaken,
nor his children begging bread. (Psalm
37:25)

Throughout the pages of the Bible there is overwhelming evidence to support the fact that God has provided for his own throughout history. God always takes good care of those who put their trust in Him. As He took good care of His historical children He will take good care of you today. You need only dare to put your trust in Him and fix your eyes on Him. He will never let you down nor disappoint you.

But my God shall supply all your need
according to his riches in glory by Christ
Jesus. (Philippians 4:19)

Child of God, regardless of the size of your own resources, God is not limited. He has promised to meet and supply *ALL* of your needs according to the unlimited resources of His Kingdom. Never forget that God is bigger and greater than all of your needs today, tomorrow, and forever. Put your unwavering trust in the hands of the unchanging God. Things like the state of the world's economy may change but our God will never change.

God the Father has "got you covered" in all the areas of your life. I trust as you read through the pages of this book your faith will be stirred and come alive to trust and believe God for your breakthrough. Remember with God all things are possible. Therefore, regardless of what you desire God to do for you, all that is needed is your faith in His promises. Never forget that what God did for others He is waiting to do for you. Also, never forget that

If thou canst believe, all things are possible to them that believeth.
(Mark 9:23)

HAVE FAITH IN YOUR WONDERFUL FATHER WHO HAS GOT YOU COVERED!

HE IS WATCHING OVER YOU

For the eyes of the Lord run to and fro throughout the whole earth, to shew himself strong in the behalf of them whose heart is perfect toward him.
(2 Chronicles 16:9)
He will not suffer thy foot to be moved: he that keepeth thee will not slumber."
(Psalm 121:3)

In conclusion, I have great good news for you, God the Father is watching over you! That means immediately after you accepted the Lord Jesus Christ into your heart as Lord and Savior of your life, God the Father became the watchman of your life. He becomes the keeper and protector of your life and everything that pertains to you. Child of God, rejoice evermore, because God has got you covered!

Chapter 4

GOD'S INSURANCE POLICY
FOR BELIEVERS

*I pray not that thou shouldest take them
out of the world, but that thou shouldest
keep them from the evil. (John 17:15)*

The Lord Jesus Christ, before He ascended to
heaven prayed to God the Father for the disciples
and also for all who would believe the Gospel through
them. That includes you and me. He asked God the
Father to "Keep them from evil." In the pages of the
Bible we find overwhelming evidence showing it is
the perfect "will" of God to protect, secure, and keep
His children in safety. Therefore, it was no surprise
Jesus prayed to God to keep us from evil before He
ascended to heaven. There is no question about it,
there is as much evil in the world today as when our
Lord was here on earth. There are evils of sin,
disease, sickness, hopelessness, drive-by shooting,
earthquakes, flooding, fearfulness, poverty, terror,
hatred, failure, and a host of others. But I have good
news for you God the Father has got you covered by
His insurance policy. You are covered under the New
Testament Blood Covenant of the Son of God.

SATAN CANNOT DO YOU
ANY HARM HERE

God makes numerous promises, throughout the Bible, guaranteeing safety, security, and protection for every one of His children. Psalm 91 is the only chapter in which all the promises are put together in one place. I believe whole- heartedly that the Spirit of God assembled these precious powerful promises in one particular place for a purpose. I believe the main reason is so we can receive the assurance of these eternal promises of God collectively, without wavering, because each verse reinforces the next.

Many times Christians refer to Psalm 91 as "The Believer's Insurance Policy." This Psalm speaks of safety and security when one abides in the presence of God. Since this is a very popular Psalm among Christians, it will be good for us to examine it.

According to Jewish scholars, Moses authored this Psalm. In the Psalm, he describes the devout man of faith who lives with God in his heart and never leaves God's shadow. Such a man is the true hero of Jewish life to whom God pledges,

> *I will satisfy him with long life and show*
> *him my salvation. (Psalm 91:16)*

On our side of the cross on which Jesus died, we Christians have revelations concerning the Psalms that the Jews did not have. In Luke 24:44 Jesus said, *"These are the words which I spoke to you while I was still with you that all things that must be fulfilled which were written in the law of Moses and the prophets and the Psalms concerning me."* And in John 5:45-46 He said, *"Do not think that I shall accuse you to the Father, there is one who accuses you—Moses, in whom you trust. For if you believed*

Moses, you would believe me; for he wrote about me."

Once we understand the revelation that God gave to the Apostle Paul, it's clear that Psalm 91 is as much for us today as it was for Moses. Jesus was hidden from the Jews, in the Old Blood Covenant, through types and shadows and revealed to us after He paid for our redemption and came to live inside of us as born-again living temples of God. We will spend the remainder of our examination of Psalm 91 in light of the New Blood Covenant.

> Verses 1-2, *"He who dwells in the secret place of the Most High shall abide under the shadow of the Almighty I will say of the Lord, "He is my refuge and my fortress; my God in Him will I trust."*

The rich promises of this whole psalm are dependent upon one's meeting the exact conditions of the first two verses. The rest of the chapter is God moving on our behalf. The word *refuge* in Strong's Concordance is defined as " a shelter, protection, fortress; a hope; a place of trust; a shelter from storms."

In these two verses, four names of God are used to describe different aspects of His protection. (1) " Most High" shows Him to be greater than any threat we face; (2) "Almighty" emphasizes His power to confront and destroy every enemy; (3) "The Lord" assures us that His presence is always with us; (4) "My God" associates intimately with those who trust in Him.

> Verse 3, *"Surely He shall deliver you from the snare of the fowler and from*

the perilous pestilence." [The fowler is one who catches birds in a trap or snare.]

Pestilence is a metaphor significant to the Hebrews since plagues of locusts and disease were common in the Middle East. This verse speaks of sudden pestilence or attacks from Satan that came in a moment, without warning, like a plague. This pestilence is designed to crush and devour everything.

Verse 4, *"He shall cover you with His feathers, And under His wings you shall take refuge; His truth shall be your shield and buckler."*

"Under His wings" is a metaphor drawn from the imagery of a hen that protects her young with her wings; hence it expresses tender protection. Likewise, our Heavenly Father will always be ready to hide and shield us as a mother hen covers her chicks (Matthew 23:37). David prayed that God's truth would continually preserve him. *(Psalms 40:11).*

The Hebrew word for truth is 'emet.' Curiously, 'emet' is spelled with the first, middle and last letter of the Hebrew alphabet; thus the Rabbis concluded that truth upholds the first and the last of God's creation, and everything in between!

According to the scriptures, Jesus said in John 14:6, *"I am the way, the truth, and the life."* John 1:1-14 tells us the word is God and the word was made flesh, which would be Jesus during His earth walk. Psalms 119:142-160 tells us that God's word is truth. Praise God! Our hope truly is in Christ and we can stake our life on God's word!

Verses 5-6, *"You shall not be afraid of the terror by night nor of the arrow that flies by day, nor of the pestilence that walks in darkness, nor of the destruction that lays waste at noonday."*

Man is most vulnerable to sudden tragedies and misfortunes that fly at him like swift arrows, without warning. Ordinarily demons operate only in the dark and flee in the light, but the terrible destroyer lays waste even in the noonday light. But glory to God, if you put your faith in Him, fear will be banished from your heart (I John 4:18).

Verse 7: A thousand may fall at your side, and ten thousand at your right hand; but it shall not come near you.

According to Jewish scholars, the left hand's power is relatively limited. The right hand is the preferred one for performance. Therefore its strength is enhanced and it can fell ten thousand. This means that countless demons will fall before the man who is shielded by God's truth.

Another Jewish scholar explains that the man of faith is shielded from the forces of evil by a vanguard of angels at his left hand and at his right. Ordinarily, a master who controls thousands of servants is expected to sustain them, but the believer is not held responsible for the guardian angels. God alone sustains them. Therefore, they shall not approach you to demand payment. Innumerable angels have been created to protect us from countless attacking demons (Hebrews 1:14; 12:22; Revelation 4:11).

Verse 8: Only with your eyes shall you look, and see the reward of the wicked.

Jewish sources say you will see and behold the destruction of the wicked who spurned God and refused to sit in the refuge of the Most High, but they will be helpless to harm you.

Verse 9: *Because you have made the LORD, who is my refuge, even the Most High, your dwelling place,*

According to Jewish scholars, verse 9 should read this way: "Because you, the man of faith, have said, 'The Lord is my refuge,' you thereby made the Most High the dwelling place of your faith."

Although the physical body of the man of faith is on the earth, his true abode is in heaven because that is where his heart, soul, and mind are concentrated. Thus, no harm can befall him because the essence of his being is high above the affect of earthlings. We are seated at the right of the Father as recruited human spirits. (Ephesians 2:6)

Verse 10: *No evil shall befall you, nor shall any plague come near your dwelling,*

The Jewish scholars interpret this as a blessing that the evil inclination should have no power over the devout man and that he should not be frightened by terrifying dreams or fantasies. The Psalmist also blesses the man of faith with a tent so that no plague will come near him. A tent suggests a wife or a marriage relationship. Tent also signifies household. The Psalmist also includes a domestic blessing that you may raise worthy children and students, who will not shame you by acting improperly in public.

Verse 11: *For He shall give His angels*

charge over you, to keep you in all your
ways.

God commissions angels to watch carefully over the lives and interests of the faithful. (1) They take special note of all those who seek continually to dwell in the presence of God, and they guard the body, soul, and spirit of these believers. (2) The protection includes all our ways. There is no limit as long as we walk in the shadow of the almighty. They bear us up in love and give us support as we face our spiritual enemies (Ephesians 6:10-12.)

These angels are not merely guardians, but witnesses as well. They observe every action and they are destined to testify for or against the man under their protection when he comes before the Heavenly Tribunal after death.

Verse 12: *In their hands they shall bear*
you up, lest you dash your foot against
a stone.

The Jews believe that angels will hold us up with their hands and raise us up above all dangers that lurk in our path. Hands are the symbol because with our hands we perform giving to charity and doing acts of kindness. Stone refers to the obstacles strewn in a man's way. The man of faith treads a clear path, free from all such obstacles, as if the forces of nature unite in their resolve to smooth his way.

Verse 13: *You shall trend upon the lion*
and the cobra, the young lion and the
serpent you shall trample underfoot.

The original Hebrew identifies these as a large mature lion and an old vicious snake. These two creatures hate each other. When they see each other they are aroused to murderous fury. Further more, if someone tramples upon either of them the other is infuriated and poised to kill. Despite the double danger of tramping on both of them at the same time, God will be at your side and you will pass through these perils unscathed.

Jesus said in Luke 10:19, *"Behold I give you the authority to trample on serpents and scorpions, and over all the power of the enemy, and nothing shall by any means hurt you!"* And the Apostle Paul said in Roman 16:20a, *"And the God of peace will crush Satan under your feet shortly."*

> Verse 14-16: *Because he has set his love upon Me, therefore I will deliver him; I will set him on high, because he has known My name. He shall call upon Me, and I will answer; I will be with him in trouble; I will deliver him and honor him. With long life I will satisfy him, and show him My salvation.*

The reason God will deliver me is because He loves me. We need a revelation of God's love for us. These verses also list God's seven "I WILLS" that He offers us. In these the Lord himself addresses His faithful followers. Because they truly love Him, He Himself promises to come to their aid in times of trouble. The secret for receiving God's protective care is a heart that is intimately attached to the Lord in gratitude and affection. He knows who such believers are and He will be with them in trouble, hear their prayers, and give them lives full of His divine presence and provision (John 14:12-21; 15:1-10; Ephesians 3:20; John 10:10).

In the Hebrew, verse 16 is literally saying, "I will fill

out the days of the man of faith. His life will not be cut short in this world. Moreover, some men live long lives that are full of frustration and disappointment, but this man will live a satisfying, meaningful life."

In closing, two thoughts come to mind. First, God desires to display His presence to the world. We are God's living temples here on this earth under the New Blood Covenant. By God manifesting Himself through us, as He desires to do, He will certainly get the attention of the world.

Second, it is our faith in God that enables God to be manifested in our lives. Faith comes by speaking, hearing, believing and doing His word (Romans 10:17; Mark 11:23-24; Hebrews 10:23; James 2:26).

YOU CAN SPEAK YOUR WAY TO BREAKTHROUGH

But what does it say? The word is near you; it is in your mouth and in your heart: that is, the word of faith, we are preaching. (Romans 10:8)

Like all of God's provision in the New Blood Covenant, we need to personalize His word when we pray and during our communion with Him and others each day. The following is one way that Psalm 91 could be personalized and paraphrased.

I dwell in the secret place of the Most High and I abide (remain stable and fixed under the shadow of the Almighty whose power no enemy can withstand.) I say of the LORD, "He is my refuge and my fortress; my God, in Him I confidently trust." Through Christ Jesus, my family and I are delivered from the

59

snare of the fowler (the Devil) and from deadly pestilence. He covered me with His feathers, and under His wings I do trust and find refuge; His truth and His faithfulness are my shield and buckler. I am not afraid of the terror and fear of the night, nor of the arrow (the evil plots and slanders of the wicked) that flies by day, Nor of the pestilence that stalks in darkness, nor of the disasters in the morning. A thousand may fall at my side, and ten thousand at my right side; but it shall not come near me. I am only a spectator as I see the reward of the wicked, because I am in Christ and inaccessible in the secret place of the Most High. Because I have made the Lord my refuge, even the Most High, no evil shall befall me, nor shall any plague or disaster come near my dwelling; For He orders His angels to accompany, protect, guard, defend, and preserve me in all my ways, because of my obedience and service unto the Lord. His angels carry me in their hands, lest I dash my foot against a stone. In Christ, I tread upon the lion and the cobra, the young lion and serpent I trample under my feet (the Devil is defeated and I hold him paralyzed [powerless] under my feet in the Name of Jesus!) "Because I have set my love upon you Lord Jesus, you have delivered me from the power of darkness and seated me on high with you (because I understand you, and have personal knowledge of your *mercy, love, kindness and faithfulness. I know that you will never leave nor forsake me.) I call upon you Lord, and you answer me; you are with me in trouble; you deliver me and honor me. With long life you satisfy me, and show me your salvation."*

Chapter 5

REFUSING TO BACK DOWN

There is no doubt that we live in the era of express mail and two-day delivery services. We send mail by express or special delivery and obtain information detailing the exact time the mail should get to its intended destination. It is also true that we live in the era of microwave ovens. We put food in the oven and set the timer to the exact time we want the food to cook. We are a generation of people who hate to wait. We want to succeed and we want it right now. We are the generation that hates to go through the process. I completely understand all of that. But, if we are going to be all that God has destined for us to be and have all that He has purchased for us through the blood of His dear Son, we must stand tall and strong and fight for what belongs to us.

SATAN WILL OPPOSE YOU

King David wrote in the book of Psalm:

Praise be to the Lord my Rock, who trains my hands for war, my fingers for battles. (Psalms 144:1)

Why should you fight for what God has already purchased through the blood of His dear Son? Because Satan contests and fights vigorously against all God has promised. He tries to keep you from obtaining what God said is already yours. In fact he succeeds a majority of the time because God's children just pack up and leave when the Devil brings opposition their way instead of standing their ground and engaging in dirty and ugly fighting against him and his forces. Remember, God never promised us a battle free life, but He assuredly guarantees us a defeat-free life. Therefore, you must fight for what belongs to you if the Devil tries to steal your stuff. You must let the Devil and his forces know that you know your heavenly rights.

Many of us know our human rights, as guaranteed to us by the constitution of our great nation, but shockingly many children of God do not know their heavenly rights. They have not thoroughly read the constitution of God, the Bible. Throughout the Bible we find encounters and evidence that the Devil does not want us to be healthy, have peace of mind, and be prosperous and successful in our lives. No wonder King David praised God for training his hands for war and his fingers for battles. We must never forget the fact that we are at war against the Devil and his forces that oppose us on every side. As children of the Most High God, we must never forget the fact that the Lord Jesus Christ has defeated the Devil and his forces that war against us. We should also rejoice in the fact that we are fighting from the victory corner of Jesus Christ!

Therefore, whatever circumstances you face today, you should never surrender your victory position but keep on fighting for what belongs to you.

Victory will be yours if you hold your peace, stand strong and refuse to give up or surrender your ground. We must never wish for healing, prosperity, and success, we must fight the good fight of faith to get them. The children of God must never accept that it is normal to live a defeated life.

Greater is He who is in us than he that is against us. (1 John 4:4).

We must never back down, regardless of circumstances we encounter in life, because God Almighty is backing us up. Let us begin to walk and live in victory!

OBEY AND BE BLESSED

Throughout the pages of the Bible we find God always gives His children instructions and strategies for victory when they face challenges and circumstances in life. For example, when the children of Israel left Egypt and came to the Red Sea there was no natural means within their reach to cross to the other side. God gave Moses instructions and a strategy to overcome the challenge.

We find another example in the lives of the children of Israel as they journeyed from Egypt to the Promised Land. When they got to the giant city of Jericho, it seemed humanly impossible to overcome the city because it was well prepared, militarily, to withstand invaders. God gave Joshua instructions and a strategy to overcome that challenge.

Every defeat and tragedy, in our lives, is due to ignored instructions! Just as God did wonders with and for the children of Israel, by giving instructions and strategies that helped overcome numerous insurmountable challenges, even so God gives instructions and strategies in His word to help us overcome all the circumstances of our lives.

Whenever we are faced with difficulties and tribulations in life, all we need do is seek the face of the Lord. He will give us instructions and strategies that help us overcome. We find these instructions and strategies in the Bible. If we follow the instructions, given by God, victory is guaranteed. The issue and big question here is, are we willing to listen to His instructions and follow through?

There is no question about it, we run into bigger troubles and make a bigger mess when we attempt to handle the issues of our lives on our own. I have tried it and I know that the outcome was not desirable. The Lord said,

> *For without me ye (you) can do nothing.*
> *(John 15:6)*

The Lord will guide and give us instruction on how to overcome the issues of life if we let Him do it for us.

KEYS TO BREAKTHROUGH

Let's take a close look at the instructions in the eighteenth chapter of Luke's Gospel. The instructions the Lord gave us in this portion of scripture can be applied as a starting point to resolve all the issues and challenges of life.

> *Then Jesus told his disciples a parable to show them that they should always pray and not give up. He said: in a certain town there was a judge who neither feared God nor cared about men. And there was a widow in that*

town who kept coming to him with the plea, grant me justice against my adversary. For some time he refused. But finally he said to himself, even though I don't fear God or care about men, yet because this widow keeps bothering me, I will see that she gets justice, so that she won't eventually wear me out with her coming. And the Lord said, listen to what the unjust judge says. And will not God bring about justice for his chosen ones, who cry out to Him day and night? Will he keep putting them off? I tell you, He will see that they get justice, and quickly. However, when the Son of Man comes, will He find faith on the earth?
(Luke 18:1-8)

What does the Lord want us to learn from this parable? There are several lessons that will help us overcome all of the circumstances and challenges of life. I believe with my whole heart that there are seven hidden victory keys that the Lord wants us to obtain. The Spirit of God has revealed them to me and I want to share them with you so your faith can be built up to believe God for the breakthrough you desperately need! I know and trust that these victory keys will turn your life around, like never before, and help you begin to enjoy the benefits the blood of the Lord Jesus Christ has already insured for you. I truly believe that these seven master keys for breakthrough can empower you to begin to live a victorious life. They will equip you with the spiritual tools you need to live triumphantly and overcome any challenges that you may be facing right now or will ever encounter in life.

THE POWER OF DESIRE

The first "Breakthrough Key" the Lord Jesus Christ want us to get out of this teaching about the widow and the wicked judge is what I call "The Power of Desire." This is a very crucial key and is the ground breaking or preparatory step for any breakthrough you may need. Do you have the desire to be blessed, move to a new level, be healed, delivered from your enemies, prosper, succeed, grow, become anointed, promoted, or to excel in all the areas of your life? If you have the "Power of Desire" for breakthrough you are on the right track to achieve it. In fact, if you are not willing to do whatever it takes to win your battles and overcome the challenges of life it is abundantly clear, throughout the Bible, that God by His nature will not impose victory on you. Child of God, there will be no breakthrough without desire to do whatever it takes to overcome the obstacle. No one can make you have the desire. You are the one to possess it within you. If you have the desire to succeed, God has the power to make it happen. The Bible tells us:

> *Delight thyself also in the Lord; and he*
> *shall give thee the desires of thine*
> *heart. (Psalm 37:4)*

From the study text, the Lord wants us to see this widow as a model for believers in the Lord Jesus Christ. This widow possessed the "power of persistent faith and determination", and believed that failure was not one of her options. The Lord wants us to learn from the parable that this widow did not merely wish for her desired breakthrough, she fought to make it happen. In other words, she possessed the desire to win. She put up some vigorous effort to see that her desired results came through. The lesson for us is that we must put our faith to work to get our desired results.

The word of God tells us that *"Faith without work is dead." (James 2:26)* We shall discuss in detail later in this chapter how to activate our faith to make great things happen. Whatever your desired breakthrough may be, all you need to do is get before the face of the living God and He will give you instruction from His word that will help you to victory. He will help you devise a strategy to make it happen. With you and God working hand in hand your breakthrough will come through.

It is incorrect, as many children of God have been taught, that God does all the work for us while we lay asleep in our beds of laziness expecting our desired breakthrough to come through. I want to challenge you to arise, as this persistent widow did and do something to achieve the breakthrough you desperately need. Work with God to make your desires come through.

As we saw from this lesson concerning the widow and the wicked judge, the Lord wants us to learn that she possessed not only the "power of persistent faith and determination" and the "Power of Desire" she also rose up and fulfilled some undesirable and tedious tasks by continuously going to the home of the wicked judge to have him grant her desired justice. Therefore, whatever your needs may be, God is able to meet those needs but you must cooperate and work with God to see your desires come through.

THE POWER OF PERSISTENT PRAYER

The second "Breakthrough Key " is what I call the "power of persistent prayer." Recall that the Lord Jesus Christ began His teaching of the parable in

Luke's gospel by saying "Men (mankind) ought always to continue in prayer and not to lose faith." I strongly believe that the Lord was laying the foundation on which our victory in life must be built. Throughout His earthly ministry we find that more than seventy percent of His time was spent in solitary places seeking the face of our heavenly Father in prayer

Child of God, there is overwhelming evidence throughout the Bible showing that every successful child of God has become so as a direct result of his or her commitment to seek the face of the Lord in constant prayer. Every one that failed in life neglected to spend time in prayer before the Lord. Every child of God must strive to have a disciplined prayer life. A prayerless child of God is like a roaring lion without teeth to fight. It can leap, roar, and intimidate but has no power to devour its prey. We must be the people of God who spend the majority of our time before God in prayer.

PRAYING IS VERY HARD AND TEDIOUS WORK

I have discovered that prayer is one of the hardest tasks that I know. I'm convinced it is very tedious and highly demanding work for every child of God. We must never forget that the Devil does not want us to pray because he realizes if we take time to go before God in faith-led fervent prayer that he is totally defeated. I have discovered that it is easy to lie down on the couch watching movies for several hours without getting tired. But as soon as I go down on my knees to seek the face of God in prayer, it is amazing how it seems the heaviness of the whole wide world suddenly falls upon me. This is one of the tricky tactics of the Devil and his forces to discourage us from praying. We must resist his lies and defy his plans!

Prayer is hard work; there is no question about that, but that is where our victory lies. Satan does not want you to pray because he knows that if you take some time to pray, God the Father through His Holy Spirit will reveal to you his evil secret devices. Oh, yes, God the Father will reveal the plans of the Devil against your life and all that pertains to you. If you know the secrets devices of your enemies, then, they are rendered powerless and defeated. No wonder he does not want you to pray because he knows very well that if you do, you will be in union and fellowship with God as Adam and Eve had fellowship with God in the Garden of Eden. Being in constant fellowship with God guarantees your safety and protection from all of your foes.

There are benefits without number when you develop a lifestyle of prayer. It is hard and tedious work but it pays very high dividends. Let us invest heavily before God on our knees. Let's begin today to pray!

Whenever you are in need of anything from God, you must first of all go before Him and search out from His word what His "will" is or promise concerning that particular need or situation. The "Will" of God is in His word! You must locate the promise of God that covers your need or the breakthrough you need. Then begin to earnestly pray about those needs. Plan and strategize how to obtain the breakthrough you desperately and badly need. Then work with God to make your desired breakthrough come through.

Getting back to our text on the teaching encounter between the widow and the wicked judge, I believe she did her spiritual and natural homework in line with the word of God. Her desperate situation was turned around because she refused to back down. She did not allow natural obstacles, intimidation of the wicked judge, and other natural opposition to stop her from obtaining her desired breakthrough.

PRAYING FOR A BREAKTHROUGH CAN BE LIKENED TO SOMEONE UNDERTAKING A HUGE PROJECT

For which of you, intending to build a tower sitteth not down first, and counteth the cost, whether he had sufficient to finish it? Lest haply, after he hath laid the foundation, and is not able to finish it, all that behold it begin to mock him. Saying, this man began to build, and was not able to finish. Or what king, going to make war against another king, sitteth not down first, and consulteth whether he be able with ten thousand to meet him that cometh against him with twenty thousand. Or else, while the other is yet a great way off, he sendeth an ambassage, and desireth conditions of peace.
(Luke 14:28-32)

From this portion of scripture we find that preparation before any undertaking, even before praying, is a very crucial step for success and victory in life. You may say, "How do these scriptures apply to praying for the breakthrough I desperately need?" Thank you for asking! I will share with you a true testimony later in this chapter on how God miraculously provided our first brand new home, against all odds, to illustrate how we must plan before praying.

I have no doubt whatsoever that if not for the power of prayer I would not be where I am today, in the Lord and otherwise. There is no question that persistent, fervent, prevailing prayer does not only change things, it changes ALL things. The Apostle Paul, in one of his writings, encouraged believers and the Church as a whole to *"Pray without ceasing."* (1 Thessalonians 5:17) Therefore, it is no coincidence that Jesus started the parable of the widow and the wicked judge with an exhortation that *"we ought always to pray and not to faint."* (Luke 18:1)

Why did the Lord say that "we ought always to pray and not to faint?" I believe that the Lord wants us to understand that a well-sustained prayer life is the key to well-sustained victories and breakthroughs. Furthermore, it is obvious that the Lord wants us to learn and understand the great importance of persistent prayer's power. In addition, I believe that the Lord used this parable to teach us how to persist in fervent prayer that produces result. He teaches us to pray until we receive the breakthrough we desire from the hands of God.

We can also connect this parable with the same subject of prayer that the Lord taught His disciples and the people in Matthew's gospel, the seventh chapter and verses seven through fourteen. Here we find the Lord emphatically teaching His disciples to persist in fervent prayer. He taught that when we ask anything of God, in prayer, that we stay on our request and keep praying until we receive the manifestation from the hands of God. He wants us to seek, and knock, and also stand still until the breakthrough becomes reality from the throne room of God. Prayer is one of the ways in which we fellowship with God and also make our requests known to Him. He wants us to pray without ceasing because the more we spend time in prayer before the living God, the more fellowship time we will have with Him. The more time we spend before the living God, the more protected we become from our enemies and the more hidden things He will reveal to us. The Bible tells us,

> *He that dwelleth in the secret place of the Most High, shall abide under the shadow of the Almighty. (Psalm 91:1)*

It is an understatement to say that prayerlessness is a sin and that it signals the beginning of downfall for any true child of God. Let us vigilantly watch out and ask God for His protection from the Devil's traps of prayerlessness. It is a killer disease that every child of God must be on guard to detect and fight against!

There is no question that faith-led, fervent and prevailing prayer enables us to do anything that God our heavenly Father can do! It can make a way where there seems to be no way. Prayer is one of the weapons we have in our possession ready for use to cancel and undo all the plans the Devil and his forces unleash against our lives. A prayerful child of God cannot be easily overtaken in time of testing faith through trials and temptations. Hence the Lord said, *"Watch and pray, that you enter not into temptation: the spirit indeed is willing, but the flesh is weak" (Matthew 26:41).* Therefore, whatever circumstances you may face today, you can pray your way out of troubles and begin to live in victory. In fact, if you take time to pray, God takes time to answer your prayers!

Finally, the Lord wants us to learn from this parable that through the "power of persistent prayer", we can live a defeat-free life even in the face of every day battles. When we combine the power of our faith and the power of persistent prayer, there is no Devil in hell that is able to overcome us! Therefore, let us pay good heed to the instruction of the Lord, *"Men ought always to pray and not to faint."* (Luke 18:1)

THE POWER OF DECISION

The third important "Breakthrough Key" is what I call the "Power of Decision." It is another lesson the Lord want us to learn from the parable of the persistent widow and the wicked judge. In this teaching of the Lord, we find the widow not only possessed the "power of desire" and "the power of strategy", she also possessed the "power of decision." She went to the wicked judge and asked him to avenge her of her adversary. Remember, the Lord told us, in the story, the judge did not have the fear of God in him neither did he have regard for others. Even though she knew these things, the widow decided that she would go to him to seek justice. The Bible tells us,

> *If any of you lack wisdom, let him ask of God, that giveth to all men liberally, and upbraideth not; and it shall be given him. But let him ask in faith not wavering. For he that wavereth is like the wave of the sea driven with the wind and tossed. For let not that man think that he shall receive any thing of the Lord. (James 1:5-7)*

The widow made up her mind that she was going to get her needs met, no matter what. In the same way, we must make up our minds on the breakthrough we want God to perform for us. I have heard many children of God pray like this: "If it be your will." They confess their uncertainty about outcomes by saying: "I don't know what God is going to do about it." Some are willing to postpone action or expectations by saying: "When I get to heaven, I will have every thing I need."

It is obvious to me that those who pray like this do not understand the full meaning of the living words of God. The Bible says, *"My people are destroyed for lack of knowledge" (Hosea 4:6).*

I am convinced that if believers in the Lord Jesus Christ get hold of the revelation the Lord is showing us in this parable they will experience a manifestation of the Lord's glory like they have never seen before and in every area of their lives. To have a deeper understanding of what the Lord was teaching His disciples and other believers, let us again go over the steps this persistent widow took when she was confronted with her problem.

First, she recognized she had a problem or need. Secondly, she analyzed her problem well and created an effective strategy to solve the problem. Thirdly, she made an unwavering decision to pursue the course of action she had mapped out to solve her problem. It is a process that leads to blessings.

I want to encourage and challenge you to follow the Kingdom method the Lord wants us to understand from this parable. It is the Lord's pleasure to bless His children with everything heaven can give. For this reason the Lord taught His disciples how the Kingdom of God operates. So act on it and watch God manifest His power in your life and give you the breakthrough you desperately need, regardless of your circumstances!

I have practiced this Kingdom formula for more than twenty-eight years and it has not failed me yet! I am sure it will not fail you either, regardless of your circumstances and challenges. It is the word of the

Living God for all who will practice it!

THE POWER OF STRATEGY

The fourth "Breakthrough Key" is the "The Power of Strategy." I believe wholeheartedly that there are more crucial lessons the Lord wants us and the Church, as a whole, to learn from this parable. The story of the encounter between the widow and the wicked judge can empower and help us find the breakthrough we desperately need even in the face of seemingly inevitable defeat and failure. This persistent widow was a very wise and visionary woman who did not just wake from sleep and go down to the home of the wicked judge. I believe she planned and strategized on how she would get her need met by this man. I also believe that she prayed, planned and strategized before putting her faith to work. After she had done her homework thoroughly, both spiritually and naturally, God gave her the desired breakthrough.

LACK OF ADEQUATE PLANNING
GUARANTEES FAILURE
AND UNDESIRABLE OUTCOME

There be four things which are little upon the earth but they are exceeding wise. The ants are a people not strong, yet they prepare their meat in the summer. The conies are but a feeble folk, yet make their houses in the rocks. The locusts have no king, yet go they forth all of them by bands. The spider taketh hold with her hands, and is in the kings' palaces. (Proverbs 30:24-28)

Just like these insignificant creatures, yet very wise in all of their doings, we must do our homework and plan well. Completing these steps before action would save us a lot of headaches and troubles in life! These insects are wise because they plan well ahead of time to prevent defeat, failure, and destruction. We must emulate their strategic way of doing things. Regardless of the breakthrough we need from the hands of the living God, we must first take time to sit down and take stock about what we ask God to do for us. In other words, find out what God has to say concerning your need.

THE POWER OF FAITH

Now faith is the substance of things hoped for, the evidence of things not seen. For by it the elders obtained a good report. But without faith it impossible to please him: for he that cometh to him must believe that he is, and that he is a rewarder of them that diligently seek him. (Hebrews 11:1-2, 6)

The Lord Jesus Christ, through the Holy Spirit and the word of God enlightened my eyes of understanding to see that the fifth crucial "Breakthrough Key" is the "Power of Faith." The Lord used this story to illustrate how we should get our needs met. He teaches us a systematic way to bring our needs to God and watch Him meet them. The widow is a model for believers and the Church of the Lord Jesus Christ, as a whole. This woman did not see failure as an option because she possessed the "power of persistent faith and determination." She was a woman full of "Faith in God" who put her faith to work because *"Faith without works is dead."* (James 2:26)

What is Faith? Faith is believing God is able to do or perform what He has promised. Through faith the widow believed this wicked judge would meet her need. The Lord wants us to see, from this story, that active faith does not take "No" for an answer. Active faith accepts no "failure" even in the face of seemingly inevitable defeat and significant obstacles. The widow is model of what the Lord Jesus Christ wants us to be because she is an example of a "Faith Fighter." The Apostle Paul encourages us in one of his writings to *"Fight the good fight of faith."* (1 Timothy 6:12)

Child of God, remember that this widow had every reason in the whole wide world not to go to the palace of the wicked judge. Since it was the only way she could get her need met she made up her mind to go to him anyway. She did not allow her fear and intimidation, by the wickedness of the Judge, to rob or hinder her of the breakthrough she desperately needed. The Lord wants us to learn from this parable that she had the kind of faith that moves mountain. This is the kind of faith the Lord taught us in Mark's gospel, the eleventh chapter. If we possess this kind of God-active faith, nothing will be impossible to us and we will be able to move the mountains of sickness, fear, lack, sin, and hopelessness. They will have no choice but to obey us and move.

Another lesson the Lord wants us to learn from the widow's faith is that she had a powerful tool of faith that boldly speaks or confesses the word of God. The widow went to the palace of the wicked judge and requested that he "avenge me of my adversary." This kind of faith speaks authoritatively against whatever the mountain may be because the person believes that the word carries enough power to accomplish what it was sent forth to do.

Jesus taught His disciples, in the gospel of Luke,

the eleventh chapter and verse number one that when they pray they should "Say." The Apostle Paul also echoed the same word of exhortation in the book of Romans the tenth chapter verses number eight through ten. The Lord wants us to discover from this teaching that by our "Faith" in God we can live from victory to victory and from glory to glory every day of our lives. Our faith in the Living God through the sacrificial shed blood of His Son is our key to an every day defeat-free life.

The scripture tells us that, *"the just shall live by faith." (Romans 1:17)* Our faith is very crucial and an integral part of our walk and relationship with God because everything we are and have comes by our faith in the living God We receive our salvation, healing, peace, joy, anointing, deliverance, the Holy Ghost, and belief that we are going to spend eternity with God in heaven all by faith in God, through the name of His dear Son.

Finally the Lord wants us to learn from this parable that by faith we can overcome all the challenges the Devil may throw our way. Furthermore, the Lord wants us to learn from this parable that *"Without faith it is impossible to please Him, for he that cometh to God must believe that He is, and that He is rewarder of them that diligently seek Him" (Hebrews 11:6).*

Recall the saying of the Lord from the above parable *" When the Son of Man cometh, shall He find faith on earth?"* Therefore, whatever may stand in our way that prevents us from enjoying fully the *"more abundant" life (John 10:10),* the Lord Jesus purchased for us, is a mountain that can be removed by our unwavering faith in the living God.

So, Child of God, I want to encourage you to have faith in the living God and begin to speak and command your mountain to go into the pit of hell. Do so in the matchless name of the Lord, Jesus Christ.

Your mountains will go if you faint not from speaking and commanding them to leave.

Suppose you have an uninvited guest who suddenly shows up at your home and you really don't ever want to see that face in your home. What would be your reaction? I think you would use every legal force available to evict that person. In the same manner you may deal with unwanted circumstances that intrude such as sickness, fear, poverty, failure, hopelessness, and all the other difficult challenges of life. It is your right to forcefully command the Devil and his agents to depart and never return again

You may say you don't have a big enough faith to move a mountain, but that is not true! The Bible says that *"God hath dealt to every man the measure of faith"* (Romans 12:3) Further, the Lord Jesus Christ never required us to have a monster faith but exhorted us to have faith *"like a mustard seed." (Mark 11:22-25)* All we need to build up our faith is the word of God. The Bible declares in the book of the First Corinthians, the tenth chapter and seventeenth verse *"So then faith cometh by hearing and hearing by the Word of God." (Romans 10:17)* The more time we spend with the Lord, dining from His table and feasting on His word, the more faith we have.

THE POWER OF PERSISTENT DETERMINATION

The sixth important "Breakthrough Key" is the "Power of Persistent Determination." Blessed are those who possess the "will and drive" to persevere for they shall experience unlimited victories in life! If we are going to have our needs met or obtain the breakthrough we desperately need or if we are to be all that God made us to be and live defeat-free lives we must learn to stand our ground, even in the face of sickness, disease, pain, hopelessness or other circumstances. We must work with God to see our desires and breakthroughs come through.

Let us take another look at what she did that brought her desired results into reality. The Lord said that she went to the palace of the wicked judge continuously to have him grant her needs. She put the power of her faith, as we discussed earlier, into action. When the judge saw that she refused to take "No" for an answer, he had no choice but to grant to her her desired result. She got her breakthrough!

Let there be no misunderstanding here concerning the Lord's intention in this parable. He was not teaching us that we should put pressure on God the Father in order to have our needs met. Far from that! He wants us to live by the faith of God on a daily basis because *"For without faith it is impossible to please God."* (Hebrews 11:6)

Believers and followers of the Lord Jesus Christ are the adopted children of Abraham. Like father, we children must live by faith, on a daily basis, as Abraham did and obtain the same good reports. Therefore, whatever your needs may be right now, I encourage you to have faith in God, rise up and take your circumstances on head to head by faith. You will be amazed what the Lord will do on your behalf.

THE POWER OF EXPECTATION

The seventh and final "Breakthrough Key" the Lord wants His disciples and church to learn from this parable is what I call the "Power of Expectation." The Lord wants His children to understand that it is not good enough to have faith to pray to God, concerning our needs or the breakthrough we seek. He wants us also to put our faith to work. He wants us to bring all of our needs to God the Father, in persistent, fervent, prevailing prayers with great expectation. If we pray without expecting God to respond to our request our prayer to God will be incomplete and disconnected.

For example, how prudent would it be if a young boy sees his father with a loaf of bread, approaches his father and requests a piece of bread but does not expect his father to favorably respond? Wouldn't it be odd if the young man, after asking turned his back to his father and folded his hands? It would be odd because the young boy failed to position himself to receive a piece of the bread.

How foolish would it be for a farmer to labor very hard during the planting season and expect no crops come harvest season? Therefore, when we come boldly before the throne of our heavenly Father and make our requests known to Him in prayer, we must never fail to position ourselves with great expectation to receive the response.

The "Power of Expectation" is an integral part of the breakthrough we desperately need. The Lord wants us to learn a valuable lesson from the widow. Her expectation carried her through the disappointment and to a successful outcome. Our loving God is much bigger and greater than all other gods combined. Let us approach His throne of grace with all our needs, in confidence, and expect Him to meet those needs according to His unlimited riches in glory!

OUR TESTIMONY

When my wife and I were residing in the northern part of Minneapolis, Minnesota and desired to own our own house. We unleashed the "power of desire." Our home church, at that time, was located in Bloomington, a southern suburb of Minneapolis. Our first concern was not about how we could secure the thousands of dollars we needed to purchase a brand new home, but for safety and access for our children who were heavily involved in the Church's youth program.

We began to seek the face of God asking in which community we should build our new home by applying the "power of prayer." After lots of prayers for direction and guidance from God, my wife and I came to the conclusion that Bloomington was the right place for us. We had the Spirit of God's inner witness that this was the right place for us. We then invoked the "power of decision."

After we settled the issue of location we began to ponder how to purchase a piece of land on which we could build our home. The "power of planning and strategy" was set in motion. The odds were against us because there were but a few pieces of land left to be developed in the City of Bloomington. Those pieces of land were terribly expensive and out of our financial reach. Securing a piece of land in Bloomington did not look good for us. But we stayed on course seeking the face of God and asking for His favor and breakthrough.

As we earnestly prayed and sought the face of God, the Holy Spirit guided us by bringing people into our lives to make our desire happen. As we persevered in fervent prayer, strategically planned, and worked with God, our breakthrough came through in the early months of 1997. The "power of faith, determination, and expectation" were put into motion at this junction. To the amazement of many who had told us that it was impossible to secure a piece of land in Bloomington on December 31, 1997, we moved into our first new home. Praise God!

Another example in the Bible, to further illustrate the importance of these crucial steps to breakthrough, can be found in the encounter between

King David and the Philistine troops who came to war against him. (1 Sam 30: 1-8). I urge you to read it.

If we seek, pray, strategically plan, and get prepared to work with God, God will guide us and assuredly bring a solution to whatever problem we face. We must be wiser than the children of the world! We must give God something to work with! As God's responsible children, we must never go to God empty handed. When we go to God in prayer we don't have to beat around the bush. By doing our homework and planning well ahead of time, it enables us to present our petition with specifics and ask in faith.

By this I mean that whenever confronted with the issues of life take them to God in prayer for guidance and direction. It works regardless of the nature of the breakthrough that you may need. The Spirit of God has given me this revelation for many years now and it has turned my life from constant defeat into constant victory. I believe that this revelation can also turn your life around.

Chapter 6

DISCOURAGED? PUT YOUR FAITH TO WORK

Why art thou cast down, oh my soul? and why art thou disquieted within me? Hope in God: for I shall yet praise him who is the health of my countenance, and my God. (Psalm 43:5)
And Ahab told Jezebel all that Elijah had done, and withal how he had slain all the prophets with the sword. Then Jezebel sent a messenger unto Elijah, saying, So let the gods do to me, and more also, if I make not thy life as the one of them by tomorrow about this time. And when he saw that, he arose, and when for his life, and came to Beershebam which belongeth to Judah, and left his servant there. But he himself went a day's journey into the wilderness, and came and sat down under a juniper tree: and he requested for himself that he might die; and said, it is enough, now, O LORD, take away my life; for I am not better than my

fathers. And as he lay and slept under a juniper tree, behold, then an angel touched him, and said unto him, Arise and eat. (1 Kings 19:1-5)

My dear friend, are you in a state of discouragement and hopelessness because of difficult circumstances and other issues of life that you are facing right at this moment? Are you contemplating packing up and surrendering your life's dreams, vision, and aspirations? Have life's issues dealt you a big blow, knocked you down and left you with a wounded heart? If that is the case, I have good news for you. Your breakthrough is around the corner! None of us is immune from discouragement and hopelessness, at one point or the other in our lives. It is a fact of life. So, give yourself a break when you are down and almost out.

Always remember that the darker the night the sooner the next day's sunshine approaches. The Lord has sent me, via the pages of this book, to encourage you with His words. You can put your faith to work and be blessed. It is your faith that can make you whole!

The Spirit of the living God led me to the above portions of the word of God to strengthen your spirit and stir up your faith so you can believe and trust God for the breakthrough you desperately need today. In these scriptures, we find King David and Elijah, great, honorable, and powerful anointed men of God in one of the lowest states of their entire lives. Both men were discouraged and hopeless.

We see that both men were faced with difficult and challenging issues of life. I have been in such hopeless conditions many times in my own life. I fully understand the pressure and heavy temptation that comes upon us when we are in such situations. When we find ourselves in a miserable state, there is a heavy pressure and temptation to surrender, pack up, and run as in the case of Elijah. But as we can see, even in their lowest and darkest hour God came to their rescue. Praise the Lord! Even so, the Lord is aware of all that you are going through right now. He knows your hiding place and He will be right there to rescue you, as well. Remember the sooner you put your faith and trust in God for deliverance, the quicker you get out of your trouble and valley. I learned this principle a hard way!

FAITH IS OUR VEHICLE TO VICTORY

Faith is the substance of things hoped for, the evidence of things not seen. For by it the elders obtained a good report. But without faith it is impossible to please him, for he that cometh to God must believe that he is, and that he is a rewarder of them that diligently seek him. (Hebrews 11:1-2, 6)

According to this portion of scripture, faith is simply believing that "God is." If we really believe that He is, then we will believe what He says. If we really believe what He says, then we will do what He says and we will be rewarded with answered prayer!

Faith is a very crucial element of our walk and relationship with God because "without Faith" we cannot please Him. How can someone walk and have a good relationship with one whom he cannot please? It is impossible! Therefore we must have "Faith" in order to be the people of God. The scripture tells us that as the elders [our brethren of old] obtained a good report [victories], so much so must we be the people of faith if we desire to obtain good reports in our lives. This means that without faith it is impossible to obtain a good report [victory].

There is no question about it! As fish cannot survive and be alive without water even so we cannot be the people of God without faith. That is because who we are, shall be, and everything we have are all by faith.

Faith can also be described as a spiritual law. The spirit world is governed by "spiritual laws" just like the physical world is governed by "physical laws." These laws operate constantly whether we understand them or not. These laws will work for us or against us, depending on how we respond to them. For example, the physical "law of gravity" can bring life or death depending on how we respond to that law. Likewise, the spiritual "law of confession" can bring life or death to us depending on how we respond to it, with our tongue! (Proverbs 18:21).

Faith is not a very difficult subject and relatively easy to develop in our lives if we so desire.

ONLY YOUR FAITH CAN MAKE YOU WHOLE

And a certain woman, which had an issue of blood twelve years, And had suffered many things of many physicians, and had spent all that she had, and was nothing bettered, but rather grew worse, When she had heard of Jesus, came in the press behind, and touched his garment. For she said, If I may touch but his clothes, I shall be whole. And straightway the fountain of her blood was dried up; and she felt in her body that she was healed of that plague. And Jesus, immediately knowing in himself that virtue had gone out of him, turned him about in the press, and said, Who touched my clothes? And his disciples said unto him, Thou seest the multitude thronging thee, and sayest thou, Who touched me? And he looked round about to see her that had done this thing. But the woman fearing and trembling, knowing what was done in her, came and fell down before him, and told him all the truth. And he said unto her. Daughter, thy faith hath made thee whole; go in peace, and be whole of thy plague. (Mark 5:25-34)

Throughout the ministry of our Lord Jesus Christ, the Bible tells us how He went about doing good and healing all that were oppressed by the Devil. It is obvious that every one the Lord healed, delivered, or blessed was as a result of their faith in the Lord. We can find Jesus saying over and over such words as "Thy faith has made you whole" (Mark 5:34) and "Let it be to you according to your faith." (Matthew 15:34) There is no doubt the same statements apply today.

The encounter in the scripture passage above took place during one of the Lord's ministry trips to the country of the Gadarenes. The verses tell us of a

91

meeting between the Lord and a woman who had an issue of blood for twenty years. We learn that this woman had suffered much at the hands of many physicians and had spent everything that she had to find a cure, but to no avail. In fact, we learn that her condition grew worse instead of better. Based on everything we learn about this woman, we know that she was in a very terrible and difficult situation. The scripture tells us that one day, she heard about the ministry and fame of the Lord Jesus Christ. The Bible says, *"So faith cometh by hearing and hearing by the word of God" (Romans 10:17).*

Child of God, there are a few things that I discovered from these portions of the words of God, concerning this woman, that we can apply to circumstances we may encounter in life. Note that she had gone through a lot of trouble, due to her illness, for twelve long years. Not only that, she had spent everything she owned to get well but to no avail. In addition, this woman had suffered many things with many physicians to get well but had no success.

Do the elements of this woman's story speak to what you may be going through in your life today? Have you done everything you know how to do to improve your life, but with no success? I have good news for you there is hope!

Based on what the scripture tells us about this woman, she had every reason in the world to pack up and quit trying to get well. She had every opportunity in the world to give up. But not this woman! She is a fighter who refused to take no for an answer. Right in the middle of her despair, she heard about the healing ministry of our Lord Jesus Christ.

There are four crucial steps that this woman took to make her healing breakthrough possible. First, she heard of the healing ministry of the Lord Jesus Christ.

The Bible says, *"So then faith cometh by hearing and hearing by the word of God" (Romans 10:17).* When she heard of the Lord her faith in what she heard began to respond and grow. All any of us need for the breakthrough we desperately need is a word from God.

Second, she said to herself, "If I may but touch his clothes, I shall be whole." She did not only hear about our Lord's healing ministry, she decided to act on what she heard by confessing what she believed would happen when she touched the hem of the Lord's clothes. The Bible says,

> *But what saith it? the word is nigh thee, even in thy mouth, and in thy heart: that is, the word of faith which we preach. That if thou shalt confess with thy mouth the Lord Jesus, and shalt believe in thine heart that God hath raised Him from the dead, thou shalt be saved. For with the heart man believeth unto righteousness; and with the mouth confession is made unto salvation. (Romans 10:8-10).*

This woman believed what she heard and confessed her desired result before she even came in contact with the Lord. That is faith at work! Recall what the scripture says, *"Faith is the substance of things hoped for the evidence of things not seen." (Hebrews 11:1).*

Third, she arose and went to find the Lord. She put feet under her faith. And fourth, she fought against obstacles and pressed her way to her desired breakthrough. I believe with all of my heart that the steps this woman took to obtain her breakthrough still apply today, regardless of the circumstances we face.

These steps I call the "Pathway to Breakthrough" can be applied, by faith, to any circumstance and they will work if we put our faith and trust in the unchangeable God. Therefore, whatever you may be faced with today all you need to obtain the breakthrough you need is faith in God.

The Bible says, "Jesus Christ is the same yesterday, and today, and forever." (Hebrews 13:8) What the faith of this woman did for her can be done for you. There is no question that whenever we purpose in our heart to fight and press for the breakthrough we need from God, the Devil uses everything within his power to fight against us and hinder us. We must be prepared to fight and oppose forcefully anything the Devil and his forces bring to bear.

I want to encourage you, by the authority of the word of God, to arise and put your faith to work. This woman did not sit lamenting, whining, complaining, and weeping over her undesirable physical condition. She did something about it and her breakthrough came.

There is another interesting lesson in this faith-building portion of the word of God. It is that this woman initiated her miracle healing and not the Lord. Child of God, if we desire to obtain the breakthrough we desperately need and live a defeat free life we must walk, act, talk, move, and fight the good fight of faith.

We can find several other examples in the Bible to show how ordinary men and women initiated their breakthrough as a result of faith in the Lord. A ruler of the Synagogue, named Jairus received the breakthrough he desperately needed when he stepped out by faith and came to the Lord Jesus Christ with his heavy load.

And, behold, there cometh one of the rulers of the Synagogue, Jairus by name; and when he saw him, he fell at his feet. And besought him greatly, saying, My little daughter lieth at the point of death: I pray thee, come and lay thy hands on her, that she may be healed; and she shall live.
(Mark 5:22-23)

Not only that, four friends received the breakthrough they desperately needed for their friend because they stepped out, by faith, and came to Jesus. The Bible tells us,

And again he entered into Capernaum after some days; and it was noised that he was in the house. And straightway many were gathered together, in so much that there was no room to receive them, no, not so much about the door: and he preached the word unto them. And they come unto him, bringing one sick of the palsy, which was borne of four. And when they could not come nigh unto him for the press, they uncovered the roof where he was: and when they had broken it up, they let down the bed wherein the sick of the palsy lay. When Jesus saw their faith, he said unto the sick of palsy, Son, thy sins be forgiven thee. (Mark 2:1-5).

These people came to the Lord Jesus Christ with their friend and were not disappointed. He healed him and gave them rest. Jesus is *"no respecter of* persons" (Acts 10:34), He will do for you what He did for others if you take the initiative and come to Him. The Bible says, "Come unto me, all ye [you] that labor and are of heavy laden [under heavy load], and I will give you rest" (Matthew 11:28).

Why not give the Lord Jesus Christ a chance today? Bring all your heavy loads to him and you will be amazed what the Lord will do for you. You may have tried everything you know to obtain the breakthrough you need but to no avail. Don't be discouraged, there is hope. Our Lord Jesus Christ is able to turn any situation around. He did it for the woman with an issue of blood when she took the initiative and helped the others who stepped out by faith and came to Him. She was not disappointed! Jesus Christ will not disappoint you either if you have the faith to believe He has the power and anointing to make you whole. Therefore, don't you dare give up! The breakthrough you desperately need from God is around the corner.

Since we cannot receive anything or please God without faith, we must therefore do everything by the grace of God to live, walk, fight and protect our faith on a daily basis. Our faith is crucial to our successful walk and relationship with God. We must strive to feed our faith with the words of God, daily, to ensure that we live from victory to victory and glory to glory. Thanks be unto God who has got us covered with His Holy Spirit to help us be the faith people of God. It is the person of the Holy Spirit that helps us live in faith.

HOW TO PROTECT YOUR FAITH

My son, attend to my words; incline thine ear unto my sayings. Let then not depart from your eyes; keep them in the midst of thine heart. For they are life unto those that find them, and health to all their flesh. Keep thy heart with all diligence; for out of it are the issues of life. (Proverbs 4:20-23)

Since our faith is crucial to our walk and relationship with God, it is very vital that we do everything we can to protect our faith from the relentless attack of the Devil and his forces. One of the biblical methods to protect our faith in God is to feed our faith with the word of God, as the above portion of scripture clearly exhorts us to do. We must constantly feed our faith with the word of God both by studying and hearing it. In other words, we must wrap our faith in the word of God. We must strive to protect our faith because our walk and relationship with God, our livelihood, and success or failure depend wholly on our faith in God. There are additional tools to effectively protect our faith. Let us take a closer look at them.

AVOID DITCHES

According to Matthew 7:13-14, there is a way of life and a way of death. The roads lead to life and the ditches lead to death. God's "will" for us is to stay on the road and out of the ditches!

The Devil cannot create anything; all he can do is pervert what God has already created. He has perverted life to death, health to sickness and disease, prosperity to poverty, and liberty to bondage to mention just a few. For example, if one were to say that the so-called "prosperity message" is a cult and of the Devil, that would be wrong. The Devil cannot create anything! God is the author of prosperity. The Devil has simply perverted this truth of God's Word and tries to get people into one of two ditches.

One of his ditches leads people to say money is evil and we must live in poverty to be spiritual. The other ditch leads people to choose making money and material things the god of their lives. God says, "Stay on the way." His way is to prosper us in every area of life. In order to do so, one must first prosper spiritually. We must give Jesus first place in our lives. Then we will truly prosper in all that we do.

WALKING IN THE SPIRIT

If we live in the Spirit, let us also walk in the Spirit. (Galatians 5:25

In Galatians 5:16, the Apostle Paul commands us to walk in the Spirit. Many people have a preconceived idea of what walking in the Spirit means. They usually describe someone who walks in the Spirit as one who spends much time in prayer, becomes a Bible scholar, has visions, or manifests any of the many "gifts of the Spirit" in their lives. But manifesting all of these things does not necessarily mean that a person is walking in the Spirit. Many times what appears to be the "Holy Spirit" is nothing more than works or emotional expression or just plain fleshly action!

According to Galatians 5:22-23, we see what is commonly referred to as the "fruit of the spirit," is also provided as our guide or standard for walking in the Spirit. In other words, if we are really walking in the Spirit, there will be love, joy, peace, longsuffering, kindness, goodness, faithfulness, gentleness, and self-control in our lives. This is what walking in the Spirit is all about! Once we experience this fruit we will not have a problem seeing the real manifestations of the Holy Spirit in the Body of Christ. We won't have to try and work something up, God's power will just flow!

AN HONEST HEART

*An honest heart is imperative in order
for God's Word to work effectively in our
hearts (Luke 8:15).*

Just because one professes to be a Christian does not mean that they have an honest heart. The Apostle James talks about born-again Christians "deceiving themselves." This is a real problem in the Body of Christ. Many Christians are not honest with God, themselves, or with others. Consequently, the Devil has many opportunities to destroy individuals, marriages, families, churches, and nations.

BE LED BY THE SPIRIT

*For as many as are led by the Spirit of
God, they are the sons of God.
(Romans 8:14).*

Jesus tells us in John 10:3-5 that His sheep know His voice and will follow Him. We live in a day where one can very easily fall into error and make all the wrong decisions in life if he or she does not know how to be led by God's Spirit! To be successful in our Christian walk, we must be led daily by the Spirit of God. We must know what it means to be led forth with peace (Isaiah 55:12). These are trying times. We must know God's voice!

RESISTING TEMPTATION

Temptations are "common" to the human race. Temptation in itself is not sinful but how we respond to temptation makes the difference. According to

James 1:14, when we are drawn into temptation, we have no one to blame but ourselves. It is our own sinful desire that tempts us and motivates us to do wrong. Once we yield to the temptation, we become "ensnared" or "trapped" and Satan has an open door to bring destruction to us. We must know who our enemy is and how he works. Then we can use the Word of God against him and flee from temptation. Otherwise, our faith will be destroyed.

LOVE AND FORGIVENESS

Not only is a walk of love and receiving forgiveness the primary way in which we protect our faith, but God also expects us to manifest the same spirit of forgiveness to anyone who has offended us. In reality, God's love and forgiveness is extended to them through us. What a privilege it is to live a life of love and forgiveness!

BIBLICAL SUBMISSION

This is another subject that can be very controversial because of all the extremes and abuses that have been experienced in the Body of Christ due to selfish and carnal applications. However, when we examine the subject fully, we see that there is biblical submission and it is necessary in order for our faith to be protected.

Men's traditional teaching on this subject usually puts women in bondage and prevents them from entering ministry. The men usually end up being little "Hitlers," whether at home or in the pulpit.

Again, if we do not understand that we are spirit beings, have souls, and live in physical bodies we will not fully understand any part of God's Word properly. This is particularly true of understanding biblical submission. For starters, we are clearly told there is neither male nor female in the spiritual Body of Christ.

God is orderly and He has established a system of headship and submission in order that things may be accomplished smoothly in homes, churches, and businesses. He instructs us in the way in which we submit to one another (Ephesians 5:21). It is not scriptural for anyone to dominate anyone in the Body of the Christ.

As we look at Ephesians 5:21-33, we can see exactly how the local church should be governed by looking at the Christian marriage. In short, we see in verse 22 that wives are to be submissive to their own husbands, making them complete even as the church, or the Bride of Christ, submits to Jesus and makes Him complete. The husband (verse 23 and 25) has a dual role. First, as the head of the marriage relationship, he represents Christ even as the local pastor represents Christ as the head of the local church. This arrangement does not negate equality. It simply means that in God's plan, one person must make final decisions or there will be confusion. Just because the husband is the head does not mean that he is superior to his wife. In fact, his wife may be more intelligent and spiritual than her husband, but he is still the head.

Secondly, the husband is to love his wife even as Christ loves the church. Well, how does Christ love his Bride, the church? According to Matthew 10:28, husbands are to be willing to die for their wives as Christ was willing to die for His Bride. It is also means that a husband becomes a servant to his wife even as Christ has come to serve His Bride. Glory to God! The truth of the teaching is that we must submit to one another!

Headship and submission is God's way for

husband and wife, pastor and local church, Jesus and his church (Bride) to work side by side mutually sharing the responsibilities of life together (Mark 16:20). God's way always works! Headship and submission, God's way, will only work where love prevails and people esteem others better than themselves.

PERSEVERANCE

Hebrews 12:1-2 and other scriptures make reference to our Christian walk as that of running a foot race. In the mind of every runner, the temptation to quit is always present. The runner must fight feelings of fatigue and the possibility of failure. But nothing should stop the runner from completing the course. Likewise, Christians often become easily discouraged. They are tempted to slow down or give up. But believers must not quit. They need to endure and through Christ, they can!

To *persevere* means "to continue doing in spite of opposition or difficulty." Hebrews 12:16 tells us to run the race with patience and endurance. The Greek word is *hypomone,* which means "the determination to muster something." It is this kind of determination that we as Christian need in order to make God's Word a reality in our lives and for our faith in Him to be protected.

Chapter 7

HOW TO GET BACK WHAT THE DEVIL HAS STOLEN

> *And I will restore to you the years that the locust hath eaten, the cankerworm, and the caterpillar, and the palmerworm, my great army which I sent among you. And ye shall eat in plenty, and be satisfied, and praise the name of the Lord your God, that hath dealt wonderously with you: and my people shall never be ashamed.*
> *(Joel 2:25-26)*
> *The thief [Devil] cometh not, but for to steal, and to kill, and to destroy: I am come that they might have life, and that they might have it more abundantly.*
> *(John 10:10)*

There is overwhelming biblical evidence to support the charge that the Devil's mission is to steal God's blessings. He wants to kill you, take all that pertains to your life, and destroy everything you have in your possession. In fact, everything that the Devil and his agents have was stolen from children of God. The

Devil has nothing of his own to brag or boast about, he is a thief and a robber!

I do not know what the Devil and his forces may have stolen from you. He may have stolen or destroyed your life by taking your health, family, peace, joy, future, hope, vision, or dreams. But, I have good news for you! God the Father, who has got you covered through the blood of His dear Son, wants to restore you beginning this moment. Our God is a God of right now. His name is I AM THAT I AM!

BEWARE OF SATAN THE GREAT DECEIVER

One of the lies that the Devil and his forces have told and caused many millions of people to believe is that whatever evil or tragedy happens to them is caused by God. That is not true! It is a lie from the pit of hell! I have had the opportunity of ministering to many people from all walks of life. Most of these lovely people were plagued with one terrible and difficult illness in their lives. These lovely people had been wrongfully taught that their undesirable physical condition was God's way of making them humble. They have been taught to believe that whatever evils, problems, troubles, and other undesirable difficult situations they faced were brought upon them by God. Tragically, the ruler of darkness, the father of all lies, the Devil, has used this lie to place and keep millions of people in bondage for years. The Bible tells us,

> So then faith cometh by hearing and hearing by the word of God.
> (Romans 10:17)

There is no question about this paradox. Faith

comes by hearing the words of God, just as fear and unbelief comes by hearing the words and lies of the Devil. You may have heard some people say: "God is the author and source of my troubles, physical impediment, and problems because He is all-knowing and powerful." They say, "Why will a loving and caring God allow His creatures to suffer?" They go on to lament, "If God is really a loving God, why does He allow evil and tragedy to happen?"

My compassionate reaction to those lovely people is that they lack full knowledge of God's powerful words. Shockingly enough, most of these people identify themselves as Christians and accept their undesirable physical condition as a way of life. The word of God state that,

> *My people are destroyed for lack of knowledge: because thou hast rejected knowledge, I will also reject thee, that thou shall be no priest to me: seeing thou hast forgotten the law of thy God, I will also forget thy children.*
> *(Hosea 4:6)*
> *And ye shall know the truth, and the truth shall make you free. (John 8:32)*

The people I meet are good people and have two prominent problems. First, they lack knowledge of the powerful words of God and second, they have been wrongfully deceived into believing the deplorable conditions they find themselves in were caused by God. These good people are taught, by so-called religious leaders of our day, that it is okay to suffer miserably here on earth.

Recently, after watching our power-packed television program the "Hour of Restoration," a young Minnesota couple decided to leave their old

105

church and began attending our Church. They left their old church because their Pastor had told the young woman that she should learn how to cope with a disease that had plagued her body for many years. When this young couple began to attend our church we showed her, from the word of God, that it is God's will to heal her body. Since they started attending our Church her failing condition drastically changed for the better. Praise the Lord! God Almighty healed her body! We did not perform any human miracle on the young woman. All we did was point her to the fact that her healing had already been paid for on the Cross of Calvary, where Jesus Christ died in her stead, more than two thousand years ago. I thank God that her faith has made her whole!

Getting back to our discussion, it is astonishing that millions of people are deceived into believing that God is the source of the problems and troubles in life. I have good news for them and for you, dear reader. The scripture above clearly states that "my people are destroyed for lack of knowledge." Since this is true, the only way God's people are going to be completely delivered, blessed, and be all that God has destined for them to be is to know the truth of God's words.

The Bible also clearly states that "Ye [you] shall know the truth, and the truth shall make you free." (John 8:32) It is my sincere prayer that this book provides you with the revelation that God's word has the power to set you free in all areas of your life. It is God's "Will" to set you free from sickness, disease, pain, hopelessness, fear, poverty, and from all the works of the Devil and his forces. Everything that pertains to life and godliness has been paid for with the blood of Jesus Christ, for you and every one who will believe on the Lord. Therefore you and I have no business living in bondage any longer! The blood of the Son of God has delivered us from the dominion of the Devil. Let us begin to enjoy and live a defeat free life.

GOD WANTS TO RESTORE YOU

As I pointed out earlier, it is the mission of the Devil to put God's people in bondage and keep them there. The Bible clearly states:

> *The thief (devil) cometh not, but for to steal, and to kill, and to destroy: I am come that they might have life, and that they might have it more abundantly.*
> *(John 10:10)*

My goal in this chapter is to place you before God the Father and enable you to begin taking back what the Devil and his agents have stolen from you. To do this I have to prepare and furnish you with delicious food from the word of God so you can have faith to believe God for the seeming impossibility. God Almighty wants to restore you today!

We clearly see, from the above portion of scripture, that the Devil has three missions against the people of God. Let us look again at these three missions. First, he is out to steal God's blessings from you and me. He wants to steal our family, career, future, hope and all that pertains to our well-being. His second mission is to kill our body, soul, and spirit. Third, the Devil's mission is to destroy you and me and everything that pertains to our lives. In contrast, the Bible records, over and over again God's will is to restore you to all that the Devil had stolen from you.

God the Father, through the blood of Jesus Christ, has paid all of our debt. Our God is still in restoration business. He went about, more than two thousand years ago, doing good and healing the sick. He is still doing the same today! He brought the dead back to life, restored sight to the blind, gave strength so the lame could walk, and cleansed the lepers.

Therefore, whatever circumstances you may face today, it is important to know that the Devil is the source of your problems. However, God is here to help you win in every circumstance. He is a loving and caring heavenly Father. It is the Devil and his forces that are out to steal from you, to kill and to destroy you and all that pertains to your life.

Jesus Christ came to give you life and to give it more abundantly. God the Father gave us Jesus Christ to ensure that we have health, peace, joy, happiness, freedom and above all eternal life with God. So, whatever the Devil and his agents may have stolen from you, God wants to restore them to you today. He wants to restore beginning now not tomorrow, I say now because our God is a right now God. He has shown again and again throughout the pages of the Bible that He takes great delight and pleasure when His children are restored. Therefore, by the authority of the powerful word of God, I announce to you that God is about to restore all that the Devil has stolen from you.

Let's take a look at the following promises to you and me. Have faith in the word of God. Because it is guaranteed by the blood covenant of Jesus Christ, it cannot fail.

> *Behold, I am the Lord, the God of all flesh: Is there any thing too hard for me? (Jeremiah 32:27)*

My friend, there is nothing, absolutely nothing, that is too hard for our God to do. He is very much able to restore your health, broken family, peace of mind, broken dreams, and bring your runaway children home. He is God of all flesh. There is nothing He cannot do. Oh my dear friend, I can feel the power of God flowing through my fingers as I type these words about the living God. I believe wholeheartedly that if you cry out to the Lord, right now, for restoration He will answer you and begin to manifest His power to you. Please do not limit the wonder working power of God to restore whatever the Devil may have stolen from you! He wants you to know that, *"For with God nothing shall be impossible" (Luke I:37)*

Dear reader, please never forget to give God praise and glory for the good things He is about to begin in your life as a result of the revelation you are receiving from this book. Now, get ready for more revelation!

Many years of accumulated wealth from God's word and the leading of His Spirit have given me what I am about to share with you. It will provoke you to move your faith life to a new level. I am very sure, by the authority of the word of God, that your life will not be the same again. I thank God for the revelation you are about to receive. It took me more than twenty years to receive these revelations and I offer them to you because they have turned my life around for the best.

TAKE YOUR STUFF BY FORCE

Child of God, it should not be surprising for you to know that the only language the Devil and his forces understand is force. The Devil is not a gentleman so you cannot negotiate with him to get back what he has stolen from you. Therefore, the only way to get your stuff from him is to use the authority that the Lord Jesus Christ has bestowed upon you. In His name beat him until he submits to you then you can grab all of your stuff from him. The Lord said,

> *No man can enter into a strong man's house, and spoil his goods, except he will first bind the strong man; and then he will spoil his house. (Mark 3:27)*
> *And from the days of John the Baptist until now, the Kingdom, of heaven suffers violence and the violent taketh it by force. (Mathew 12:11)*

Don't waste your precious time trying to negotiate with the Devil. Fight him forcefully and bind him in the name of the Lord Jesus Christ. Then take all your stuff from him. He is a relentless enemy who is out to destroy us so let us destroy him before he gets us.

As I mentioned earlier, the Lord has blessed me with an opportunity to minister to people from all walks of life. Many of them have asked me a most difficult and troubling question, "Why would a loving God allow evil things to happen to His children?" Many of these good folks want to know why evil things continue to persist in the world without the intervention of a loving God. My answer to this striking question can be found in the Bible. Let me say forcefully and with the authority of the word of God that He is not the architect of evil deeds that happen to mankind. The ruler of darkness, the deceiver, and the father of all lies, the Devil is the one who comes with the mission to steal, and to kill, and to destroy you and all that pertains to you.

God is a good God and all His deeds are good! Child of God, you should never forget this biblical fact! It is the Devil who terrorizes the children of God and causes all kinds of havoc against them and not God. It is very important to get this fact settled in the depths of your heart: God is good and He is good not some of the time but all the time and the Devil is bad all of the time.

Getting back to the striking question above, let's dig some hidden treasure from the wealth of God's word so we can find the answer. The Bible clearly says:

> *Be sober, be vigilant, because your adversary the Devil, as a roaring lion, walketh about, seeking whom he may devour. (1 Peter 5:7)*

As we have said, it is the mission of the Devil to rob us of that which God gives us. In the scriptures above, the Apostle Peter, by the Spirit of God, warned believers and the Church of the Lord Jesus Christ to be vigilant at all times. The Devil, who never takes any vacation, is always walking about across the earth looking for the opportunity to cause havoc. He is always looking for ways he can steal, and to kill, and to destroy. We must always be on our guard to fight the Devil and his forces whenever they try to intrude upon our lives and upon those things that pertain to us. I will share with you, later in the book, how we can use the seven weapons God has provided to prevent the Devil and his forces from interfering with our lives. God the Father has given us victory through the completed work of His Son on the Cross of Calvary. It is left for us to claim victory over the Devil and his agents.

One of the victories that believers have over the Devil and his forces is the ability, through the Spirit of God, to see the devices the Devil uses against us. God would not allow anything evil to come near His children without forewarning them. This is the most important key to victory over the Devil and his forces.

God reveals His own secrets and also the secrets of our enemies, to us. Let us discover support for this revelation in the word of God:

> *Surely the Lord God will do nothing, but he revealeth his secret unto his servants the prophets. (Amos 3:7)*
> *The secret things belong unto the Lord our God: but those things which are revealed belong unto us and to our children for ever, that we may do all the words of the law. (Deuteronomy 29:29)*

SIN IS THE ROOT OF ALL TROUBLES

There is no question that the power of sin is the source of all troubles in life. Sin came into the world through man's disobedience. It is the power of sin that opens the door to all of the Devil's attacks on us. Therefore, we must forcefully shut the door against the power of sin. In so doing, we shut the door against all the devices and attacks of the Devil and his agents. Sin and sickness are like twin brothers born from the same womb. They are interdependent. If you are successful in destroying one of them, the other is automatically rendered powerless. "But thanks be to God, which giveth us the victory through our Lord Jesus Christ." (1 Corinthians 15:57)

Our elder Brother, the Lord Jesus Christ, defeated the Devil through His sacrifice on the Cross of Calvary. In so doing He rendered the power of sin and all the consequences of sin powerless.

In the Bible, especially in the books of the Old Testament, we find that sometimes God would allow the Devil and his forces to gain access to His children. He was permitted to steal their stuff when they failed to listen to forewarnings of impending danger by their enemy. Let us check this out in the Bible and see that if we get rid of the power of sin we also get rid of the power of sickness, diseases, fearfulness, pain, hopelessness, depression, and all the troubles that come along with them.

> *And I will restore to you the years that the locusts hath eaten, The cankerworm, and the caterpiller, and the palmerworm, my great army which I sent among you. fear not, O land; Be glad and rejoice: For the Lord will do great things. Be not afraid, Ye beasts of the field: And ye shall eat in plenty, and be satisfied, and praise the name of the Lord your God, that hath dealt wonderously with you: And my people shall never be ashamed. (Joel 2:25-28)*

We see, from this portion of scripture, that sin opens doors for the Devil to attack God's children. We find that God allowed enemies to access His children's lives because their sin hardened their hearts. They failed to repent from their evil deeds and ways. If you take some time to read the entire second chapter of Joel, you will find that the children of Israel repeatedly sinned against God and failed to heed the warnings of the prophets. They provoked God to wrath by failing to repent from their evil deeds and ways.

In the first and second chapters of the book we find that God repeatedly warned the children of Israel against impending destruction if they failed to repent and turn from their evil ways. God hates sin and unrighteousness. He punishes His children, as a good father does, if they do evil deeds, with the hope of saving them from eternal destruction. We can see

113

this working throughout the Bible. When the children of Israel sinned and cried to God in repentance and for deliverance, He always rebuked the evil that came upon them and saved them from further destruction. He still will do the same. We are serving a living and loving God!

Let me quickly and carefully say that it is <u>not</u> biblically true that every attack on God's children is necessarily a result of sin and disobedience to God. I believe it is very important to point out this fact to avoid any confusion and misunderstanding. I have been through many attacks by the Devil and his forces not because I had sinned against my God but because I was doing the "Will" of God. Therefore, it is not biblical to assume that every attack of the Devil is a result of sin. Whenever a child of God is faced with life challenges our first move should be to seek the face of God concerning the situation. God will give us light to see clearly what is really going on. For example, the Bible tells us how Job went through a tough time of testing, trial and tribulation. He suffered a great deal of hardship and lost everything he had. All these things happened to him not because he had sinned against God but because he was a righteous man.

How can we then differentiate which attacks come upon us as a result of sin and which do not. The Bible has a ready-made answer for us. The Bible tells us,

Call unto me and I will answer you and
show you great and mighty things which
thou knowest not. (Jeremiah 33:3)

The Lord wants us to call upon Him should we have questions and promised to answer us and show us things we do not know nor understand. Child of God, how about that? "God's got you covered" in every area of your life. Praised be His name forever.

Let us take a look at another instance when God allowed the Devil access to His children.

> *The people of the land have used oppression, and exercise robbery, and have vexed the poor and needy: yea, they have oppressed the stranger wrongfully. And I sought for a man among them, that should make up the hedge, and stand in the gap before me for the land, that I should not destroy it: but I found none. Therefore have I pour out mine indignation upon them; I have consumed them with the fire of my wrath: their own way have I recompensed upon their heads, saith the Lord God. (Ezekiel 22:29-31)*

Again we find God allowed the Devil and his forces access to His people because they sinned against God and did not heed the warning to repent. In this event we clearly see that God was not pleased with how the children of Israel were mistreating strangers, the poor, and needy who dwelt among them. These powerless individuals were oppressed and mistreated and it displeased God. God looked among the children of Israel to see if there was any willing soul who would stand in the gap before God repenting their sin and wickedness against God. He found none and allowed the Devil and his forces access to His children's lives and everything that pertained to them. There is no question about it, sin and disobedience are the root source for all the troubles we go through today. It is equally sure that our faith in the blood of the Lord Jesus Christ, the only Son of God, is our only remedy.

Now I believe we are ready to answer the question we addressed above, "Can a loving God allow the Devil access to attack His children's lives and also steal their stuff?" The answer is conditionally, "yes." As we saw from the scriptures above, God allowed the Devil access to touch His children's lives and their stuff because they sinned against Him, hardened their hearts and neglected to return to Him in humble repentance. Remember that *"It is not God's will that any should perish, but that all should come to repentance." (2 Peter 3:9)*

My dear friend, whatever the Devil may have stolen from you, I want you to know that God is abundantly able to restore it. He has the power and everything it takes to restore you, so have faith in God.

Chapter 8

SEVEN KEYS TO RESTORATION

And I will restore to you the years that the locusts hath eaten, The cankerworm, and the caterpillar, and the palmerworm, my great army which I sent among you. And ye shall eat in plenty, and be satisfied, and praise the name of the Lord your God, that hath dealt wonderously with you: And my people shall never be ashamed.
(Joel 2:25-28)

In chapter seven, we dealt with misconceptions we have been made to believe regarding the ill-founded and un-biblical doctrine that God is responsible for the evil things that happen to us. We also laid the foundation that it is God's perfect "will" to restore all that the Devil has stolen from us. It is my earnest prayer and expectation that as you read this book, especially this chapter, that your faith would come alive to believe God for your breakthrough. I believe that God wants to give you double blessings for all the troubles, hell, and mess the Devil has taken you through.

As I have said, the Lord has given me some powerful revelations that have turned my life around for the best. I trust God, with all of my heart, that the revelations I am sharing with you will turn your life around as well. I want you to know, by the authority of God's word, that it is His perfect "will" to restore to you all that the Devil and his agents have stolen from you. It may interest you to know that Almighty God is more eager to restore all that the Devil and his forces have stolen from you than you may want them restored!

Let's look at how God restored King David and his six hundred armies all that the enemy had stolen from them. I want us to carefully study the book of First Samuel, chapter thirty beginning from verse number one through to the end of the chapter. I believe the revelation you receive will provoke and challenge you to fight to get back all that the enemy has taken from you. I also believe that it will be a great blessing to you. Get ready for a life transforming revelation!

BELIEVE THAT GOD IS ABLE TO RESTORE TO YOU ALL THE DEVIL HAS STOLEN

The first key to restoration is that you must believe God is able to restore to you all the Devil has stolen.

> *Now faith is the substance of things hoped for, the evidence of things not seen. For by it the elders obtained a good report. But without faith it is impossible to please him: for he that cometh to God must believe that he is, and that he is the rewarder of them that diligently seek him. (Hebrews 11:1-2, 7)*

118

This is an important key for every one who desires restoration by the mighty hands of the living God because the scripture clearly states that we cannot receive anything from God without faith. Faith is a very crucial element of our walk and relationship with God. It is the vehicle through which we can receive anything from God. For by it, we receive the forgiveness of our sins through the blood of Jesus Christ. By faith we also receive healing, deliverance, peace, joy, anointing, and all the good gifts that only come from God. Not only that, by faith we believe that we have a home in heaven, the kingdom of God, after our earthly journey is over. In fact, we cannot receive anything from God without faith and neither can we please God without it.

These revelations from the word of God, coupled with my encounters and experiences with God, have blessed my life and I trust will bless you as well and turn your life around for the best. The word of God says:

> But without faith it is impossible to please him: for he that cometh to God must believe that he is, and that he a rewarder of them that diligently seek him. (Hebrews 11:6)

Therefore, if you want God to restore whatever the Devil has stolen from you, you must put your trust in God and believe that He is able to do what you are asking Him to do. That is how faith works! You must believe that God is able to restore you.

> Therefore I say unto you, whatsoever things ye [you] desire, when ye [you] pray, believe that ye[you] receive them, and ye[you] shall have them.
> (Mark 11:24)

When you ask God in fervent prevailing prayer for the restoration of what the Devil has stolen from you, you must ask in faith and then the miracle of restoration will begin to manifest. It is a faith walk!

When I received these revelations many years ago and began to practice them, God restored all that the Devil had stolen from me. It did not came easily I must admit, but through the words of God, I began to train my wavering faith to believe God for my total restoration. It worked!

NEVER ALLOW THE DEVIL TO KEEP YOU WEEPING OVER WHAT WAS LOST

The second key to restoration is that you must never allow the Devil to keep you weeping over what was lost. One of the Devil's greatest weapons against the children of God is to make us focus on our troubles, tribulations, and problems. Why does the Devil work so very hard to keep us focused on our circumstances instead of looking up to God? Because he understands very well this will distract us from remembering the promises of God.

This is a noble revelation that you and I should always remember. The Devil and his forces want us to think that the circumstances we face are bigger than the promises of God. There is no question about it! The Devil takes great pleasure in magnifying whatever circumstances we face. Remember that the Bible says that the Devil is the father of all lies. If the Devil's lies convince you that you are not going to be able to overcome the circumstances you face, he has got you partially defeated. Therefore, when you are faced with difficult and challenging situations because of what the Devil has stolen from you, never allow him to keep you weeping over your losses.

Let us take a close look at the great King David

and his army of six hundred after they had lost all that they had.

> *And it came to pass, when David and his men were come to Ziklag on the third day, that the Amalekites had invaded the south, and Ziklag, and had smitten Ziklag, and burned it with fire. And had taken the women captives that were therein: they slew not any, either great or small, but carry them away, and went on their way. So David and his men came to the city, and behold, it was burn with fire: and their wives, and their sons, and their daughters, were taken captives. Then David and the people that were with him lifted up their voice and wept, until they had no more power to weep. (1 Samuel 30:1-4)*

We clearly see the tactics of the Devil at work in this portion of scripture. It is obvious that, after the Devil had stolen everything King David and his six hundred men had, he succeeded in keeping them focused on and weeping over their circumstances. I understand that when we find our selves in a situation such as King David and his six hundred men faced, our natural tendency or reaction is to do what they did, weep about our losses. That is our normal human response.

As soon as possible we must stop and take comfort in the presence of God. The fact that King David and his six hundred men wept bitterly until they had no more strength to weep was not the issue. The trick of the Devil was to keep them weeping and focused on circumstances and not on God who was eager to restore all that the enemy had stolen.

Like David and his men, you and I must guard against the deceptive tactics of the Devil and strive to be "still" or calm when we are faced with challenging circumstances. Failure to do so causes us to miss God and His saving power. The Bible says, "The joy of the Lord is our strength." (Nehemiah 8:10) The Devil realizes that if he can keep us focused on our troubles and problems it is likely we will lose our joy. When that happens our strength is gone. That is what the Devil wants!

Not only that, the Devil knows that if he can keep us focused on our troubles, circumstances, and problems then our faith in God will be weakened and replaced with fearfulness and defeat. Faith cannot operate in the presence of fear! Believers and the Church of the Lord Jesus Christ as a whole must never allow the Devil and his forces to have their way in our lives, even in the face of difficult challenges. God is able to turn any situation around. So, whatever circumstances you face right now, I want to encourage you to take your eyes off your circumstances and fix them on God.

King David was moved by the Spirit of the living God to write:

> *I will lift up mine eyes unto the hills from whence cometh my help. My help cometh from the Lord, which made the heaven and earth. (Psalm 121:1-2)*

Whatever the Devil may have stolen from you, I want you to know that God wants to restore it to you today, if you call upon Him to do so. He is a God of restoration and He wants to begin today and not tomorrow. In your circumstance, you must forcefully and boldly let the Devil know that you are down but not out. I assure you, my friend, by the authority of the word of God, you are coming out of the mess you are in now. God is about to restore you and give you a new beginning. But you must call upon Him to restore you.

IN THE MIDST OF YOUR STORM ECOURAGE YOURSELF IN THE LORD

The third key to restoration is that you must encourage yourself in the Lord while you are in the midst of your storm. One of the most vital lessons I have learned in my walk and relationship with the Lord Jesus Christ, especially when I am faced with difficult situations and issues of life, is to always take time out to seek the face of God in prayers for guidance and understanding to overcome the circumstances that I am facing. While I seek guidance and understanding, I always praise God for previous victories. This is a faith building strategy!

By praising God in the midst of my trouble, I am telling the Devil that the same God who has seen and brought me through other difficult and challenging situations will do it for me again. There is no way that I could count the previous victories and breakthroughs the Lord has brought me through. Neither could I name all the blessings of the Lord in my life and count them one by one but I have learned to always take some time to reflect on what the Lord has done for me and how He has brought me through many dangers.

Therefore, it is wise for every believer to build up their faith in the Lord by constantly remembering what the Lord has done for them. In doing so we build and stir up our faith in the Lord for the strength we need to face tomorrow.

We can see this principle at work in the life of King David and his men, even in the face of defeat and terrible destruction. Let us see what King David did when everything around him had terribly fallen apart.

> *And David was greatly distressed: for the people spake of stoning him, because the soul of all the people was grieved, every man for his sons and for his daughters: but David encouraged himself in the Lord.*
> *(1 Samuel 30:6)*

My dear friend in the Lord Jesus Christ, I want you to know that you and I serve an amazing God who is exceedingly able to turn things around regardless of how badly the situation may seem. King David's process of recovery began when he took time away from the weeping men, their burning city and the heartbreaking news of their wives, sons and daughters in captivity. I am sure that King David did not deny the fact that he and his small army were in a big trouble but he disciplined himself to look up to God for help.

In the same way, children of God must never lose sight of God even in their time of trouble because He has the power to turn our mess into a miracle, sorrow into singing, prison into palace, and fear into faith. Even when things were not going well for King David and his men, he did not lose sight of God. So must you and I keep our eyes on the Lord even when things are not as we had envisioned. I encourage you to put all of your trust in the hands of the unchangeable God. He will not let those who look up to Him be ashamed. Whatever your troubles, problems, mountains of circumstances or whatever the Devil may have stolen from you, count on Almighty God to be there for you.

IN TOUGH TIMES NEVER RUN FROM GOD, RUN TO HIM

The fourth key revelation to restoration is in tough times, never run from God, run to Him. Many children of God make the mistake of calling upon God after all other sources have failed them. I have heard Christians say something like this "Now that I have tried everything else, without any success, I think it's about time to go to God." Sometimes, my reaction to those people is to realize that they have it all wrong.

My dear Christian friend, God Almighty must always be our first call for help, not the last. Why do Christians go to God after all other sources fail? Because many have not recognized the awesome God we serve. Oh, how I pray that all children of the Most High God will get hold of this important revelation! We must entrust our lives to God, come what may. He is exceedingly able to fix any problem that we may face, right now or in the future.

In the midst of all the turmoil, King David ran to seek the face of God. The Bible records:

> *And David said to Abiathar the preist, Ahimelech's son, I pray thee, bring me hither the ephod. And Abiathar brought thither the ephod to David. And David enquired at the Lord, saying, shall I pursue after the troop? Shall I overtake them? And He answered him, pursue: for thou shall surely overtake them, and without fail recover all.*
> *(1 Samuel 30:7-8)*

As children of the living God, we must never forget that even in our darkest moments God Almighty is

125

still in control. We can clearly see, in the midst of surrounding storms, King David made the decision that he was not going down without a fight. First, he encouraged himself in the Lord. Second, he requested a worship instrument from the Priest. Then, he did what he later wrote in one of his books:

> *Enter into His gates with thanksgiving, and into His courts with praise: be thankful unto Him and bless His name. (Psalm 100:4)*

My dear reader, I pray that you would get this revelation. It will turn your life around forever. Remember that King David and his six hundred men were in the biggest mess of their lives. Their situation was so hopeless that the loyal troops even thought of stoning King David. That not withstanding, King David took time to seek the face of God who was able to save him. He went before God with thanksgiving and praises and asked God what he should do. It is very important to note that King David did not go before the face of God with complaining and weeping. He went into the presence of God singing, giving thanks and worshiping. This is exactly what the Lord wants His children to do today, even in the face of seemingly insurmountable mountains. We will never go wrong seeking the face of God concerning challenges life brings our way.

Finally, we also see that not until King David sought the Lord did the Lord give him orders to pursue his enemies and recover all that they had stolen. God promised to give him all that had been taken. My dear reader, whatever the Devil may have taken from you, I want you to know that God is able to restore them. Just call upon Jesus Christ today and He will manifest His power on your behalf!

GOD WILL GIVE YOU INSTRUCTIONS FOR YOUR RESTORATION

The fifth revelation key that the Spirit of God has given to me is that God will give you instructions for your restoration. In the Bible we find that God takes delight when His children seek His face. Let's look at a few scriptures to support this point.

> *The young lions do lack, and suffer hunger: but they that seek the Lord shall not want any good thing.*
> *(Psalm 34:10)*
> *And ye shall seek me, and find me, when ye shall search for me with all your heart. (Jeremiah 29:13)*
> *The Lord is good unto them that wait for Him,to the soul that seeketh Him (Lamentations 3:25)*
> *Call unto me, and I will answer thee, and shew thee great and mighty things, which thou knowest not.*
> *(Jeremiah 33:3)*

These portions of scripture clearly tell us that if children of God take time to seek the face of God, He will answer us and manifest His goodness and mercy to us. He also promises to show us things we don't know. That was exactly what King David did. He temporarily ignored all the turmoil that swirled around him like mighty river and sought the face of God for guidance and instruction.

> *And He answered him, pursue: for thou shall surely overtake them; and without fail recover all. (1 Samuel 30:8)*

It is obvious that all King David needed was a word from the living God. In the same way all that you and I need, regardless of the challenges that may cross our paths, is a word from God. Why a word from the mouth of God? Because there is more than enough power in the word of God to deliver, save, restore, heal, and do great things for the person or persons to whom the word is sent.

REMEMBER TO PLANT A SEED

The sixth revelation key for restoration is that you must remember to plant a seed. One of the most shocking revelations in this study of King David is that the best time to plant a seed for a future harvest is in the most difficult time we are experiencing. I have personally practiced this revelation and I boldly testify that it works one hundred percent of the time. It is my prayer that you put your faith to work and practice what I am sharing with you in this book. It will turn your life around for the best. Let's look at what King David and his men did in one of their most challenging times. The Bible says that:

> *And they found an Egyptian in the field, and brought him to David, and give him bread, and he did eat: and they made him drink water, and they gave him piece of cake of figs. And two clusters of raisins: and when he had eaten, his spirit came again to him. For he had eaten no bread, nor drank any water, three days and three nights. (*
> *1 Samuel 30:11-12)*

We clearly see here that despite the unenviable and uncertain situation of King David and his army;

they went out of their way to show mercy and sowed a seed in the life of a dying unknown Egyptian man. Because they ministered to this Egyptian man, God used the man to show King David where the enemies were. We should never forget that what goes around comes around! What you make happen to others God will make happen to you. It is God's law of seedtime and harvest. It cannot fail.

Therefore child of God, I encourage you, by the authority of the word of God, to go out of your way to sow a seed for a future harvest. Do so even in your darkest hour because in so doing you give God something to use to perform a miracle for you.

FORGIVE OTHERS, GIVE GOD PRAISE AND SHARE YOUR BLESSINGS WITH OTHERS

Finally, the seventh revelation key for restoration is that you must forgive others, give God all the praises, and share your blessings with others. The Lord wants His children to be blessed in all areas of their lives. This seventh victory key is very crucial to the other six keys discussed above. We must forgive others so that our blessings may not be hindered. Notice that as King David and his men pursued their enemies a time came when the whole army was not able to continue. Two hundred disabled warriors stayed behind while the able four hundred men went on. After they recovered all that was stolen from them they returned to meet the disabled men and disputed with them.

> *Then answered all the wicked men and men of Belial, of those that went with David, and said, because they went not with us, we will not give them ought of*

> *the spoil that we recovered, save to every man his wife and his children, that they may lead them away, and depart. Then said David, ye shall not do so, my brethren, with that which the Lord hath given us, who hath preserved us, and delivered the company that came against us into our hand.*
> *(1Samuel 30:22-23)*

King David reminded his brethren not to deal badly with the two hundred who were not able to pursue their enemies. The main lesson for the church of the Lord here is that we need to forgive one another and bear each other weaknesses as well as strengths. The Devil and his forces attempt to use whatever they can to hinder our total restoration. Let us be watchful so the enemy called "Unforgiveness" does not stand in the way of restoration. Also, we must never forget to give God all the glory when we are restored. Finally, we must share the blessings and testimony of God's wonder working power that made our restoration possible.

> *And when David came to Ziklag, he sent of the spoil unto the elders of Judah, even to his friends, saying, behold a present for you of the spoil of the enemies of the Lord. To them which were in Bethel, and to them which were in south Ramoth, and to them which were in Jattir.*
> *(1 Samuel 30:26)*

Fellow Christian friend, I want to challenge you to get up and go after whatever the Devil and his forces may have stolen from you. And God will restore them to you beginning now in Jesus powerful and mighty name, amen. Yes, you can be restored!

Chapter 9

FEAR NOT ONLY BELIEVE

Jesus said unto him, if thou canst believe, all things are possible to them that believeth. (Mark 9:23)
The fear of man bringeth a snare: But whoso puteth his trust in the Lord shall be safe. (Proverbs 29:25)

Fear is not of God but of the Devil! Throughout the pages of the Bible, we find that there are more than three hundred places where the Lord exhorts His children never to be fearful or be afraid. The Lord does not want us to live a fearful life style because fearfulness is not of God but of the Devil. Fear torments us and the Devil specializes in using the spirit of fear to deceive the children of God.

In this chapter, I want to share how you can use the power in the blood of Jesus Christ to overcome the destructive spirit of fear that has held many children of God captive and handicapped for too long. Fear is one of the Devil's strongest weapons against the children of God. The Devil uses the spirit of fear to rob us of our peace, joy, hope, future, health, relationship to God and others, strength, and many other good gifts and blessings of God in our lives. The Lord does not want us to live a fearful lifestyle because fear poisons our soul, spirit, and body.

Not only that but fear is the greatest enemy to our faith. Any child of God who constantly lives in fear cannot operate in faith and "For without faith it is impossible to please God." (Hebrews 11:6) Fear and faith can never coexist because either one of them has the power and force to dominate the other. The dominant one will eventually destroy the less dominant one. We must train our hearts to live without fear because the Lord has GOT US COVERED. The great King David confidently wrote:

> *The Lord is my light and my salvation; whom shall I fear? The Lord is the strength of my life; of whom shall I be afraid? When the wicked, even mine enemies and my foes, came upon me to eat up my flesh, they stumbled and fell. Though an host should encamp against me, my heart shall not fear: though war should rise against me, in this will I be confident. (Psalms 27:1-3)*

The Lord wants us to live without fear not only because it is poisonous and causes torment but because His covenant blood has already redeemed us from these deceptive devices. Therefore, whatever circumstances you face today you must guard your faith to prevent the Devil from attacking you with the spirit of fear. Your faith is one of the key weapons God gives you to fight the Devil and his forces.

The scriptures offer us many examples of faith conquering fear. One of the greatest and remarkable miracles our Lord Jesus Christ performed took place in the house of one of the rulers of the Synagogue named Jairus.

> *When Jesus had again crossed over by boat to the other side of the lake, a large crowed gathered around him while he was by the lake. Then one of the synagogue rulers, named Jairus, came there. Seeing Jesus, he fell at his feet and pleaded earnestly with him "My little daughter is dying. Please come and put your hands on her so that she will be healed and live." So Jesus went with him. A large crowd followed and pressed around him. (Mark 5:21-24)*

The scripture records that Jesus went to the home of Jairus to heal his little sick daughter. While they were yet on the way, the ruler of the Synagogue received heart-breaking news, from his house, that his daughter had died. When Jesus heard the bad news, He reacted this way:

> *While Jesus was still speaking, some men came from the house of Jairus, the Synagogue ruler. Your daughter is dead, they said. Why bother the teacher any more? Ignoring what they said, Jesus told the Synagogue ruler, "Don't be afraid, just believe." (Mark 5:35-36)*

Other portions of scripture give us the reason why the Lord reacted to bad news the way He did. The Bible records that:

> *Fear of man will prove to be snare, but whosoever trusts in the Lord is kept safe. (Proverbs 29:25)*

The Lord's reaction to the bad news was to protect the faith of the ruler of the Synagogue from falling apart because fear and faith cannot coexist in the same environment. He did not want dominant fear to overcome the less dominant faith and the ruler to be left with emptiness. Jesus stepped in quickly and interrupted the bearers of the bad news before the ruler reacted negatively. Isn't the Lord Jesus Christ wonderful? He is! He still offers the same wonderful favor on our behalf, today! Child of God, I encourage you to put all of your trust in the Lord! He will never let you down.

There are some great life-changing lessons in this biblical event that we should learn. The Spirit of God has revealed deeper thoughts to me that may be of great benefit and blessing to you. So, hold on tight to your seat for a great ride in the Spirit.

There are several principles at work in this extraordinary event. I pray that you grasp what I am about to share with you. You may recall in chapter four we discussed seven master keys to breakthrough. Here in our discussion, I will make use of five of those keys but from a totally different perspective to booster our faith and knowledge. I trust you will be blessed.

First, the ruler of the Synagogue had in his possession "Desire." This is the first key principle for victory in anything we may ever seek from the living God. He had desire to have his daughter healed. Secondly, he had another key principle for victory that made the miracle possible. He had "Faith." He met the Lord and invited Him home to heal his sick daughter because he had heard of the supernatural miracles Jesus performed in the region. This is very crucial because the scripture says that:

Consequently, faith comes by hearing the message, and the message is heard through the word of Christ. (Romans 10:17)

Because of what he had heard and kept on hearing about Jesus Christ, his faith rose within him. He believed that what the Lord had done for others He could do for him.

The ruler had a third key principle for victory, "Decision." It is not good enough to have "Desire" and "Faith" for something good to happen. Both "Desire and "Faith," which of course are good soil for victory, must be accompanied by relentless action to bring about the victory that the Lord destines for His children. The ruler of the Synagogue added action plans to his "Desire" and "Faith" bringing his heart desire to reality, the healing of his sick daughter. He made the crucial decision to go and seek the Lord. This is an important principle.

Let us recall what the scripture says; "Faith without work is dead" (James 2:26). Child of God, in order for you and me to breakthrough and become all that God has destined us to be, we must accompany "Desire" and "Faith" with corresponding action plans to obtain victory. We see from the ruler's encounter with the Lord that he followed these scriptural paths to victory.

Furthermore, the ruler had a fourth principle, "Persistent Determination." He made the crucial decision to seek the Lord for help. He made a long journey from the city where he lived to look for the Lord. I truly believe many challenges rose up against his decision to travel. Whatever his opposition was we see from the story that he defied them, went after the Lord and was not disappointed.

Fifth and finally, the ruler had "Expectation." He

sought the Lord with great expectation. Praise the Lord, the expectation of the Synagogue leader was not cut off. Child of God, these five spiritual principles can be applied to any circumstance regardless of how big or small it may be.

Getting back to the Lord's response concerning the death of the ruler's daughter, when the news got the Lord's attention, he responded:

> *Don't be afraid, just believe.*
> *(Mark 5:36)*

Why did the Lord make such a bold statement to a man who had just heard that his only daughter had died? Because He is God and there is absolutely nothing that is too hard for him to do. Also, He made the statement because He is the resurrection and life. Not only that, the Lord made the statement because He wanted the ruler to know that He had the situation under control.

In addition, the Lord made the statement because He knew whose He was. The Lord knew that His heavenly Father was with Him and that He would hear His prayer when He called upon Him to restore the life of the young girl. Furthermore, the Lord made the statement because He was confident and trusted His Father would back Him against any challenges.

Child of God, we serve a mighty and powerful God who promises to be with us always, even to the end of the world. Whatever you face today I want you to know, by the authority of God's word, that you will come out of your troubles victoriously.

Not only that, the Lord made that statement because He is the creator of heaven and earth and the source of all lives. In His presence the power of death is rendered void. The Lord is with you always even as He was with the ruler of the Synagogue. He says to you, right now, "Don't be afraid, only believe." Whatever you face today He is with you always to save, deliver, restore, heal, help, and bless you.

The Lord told the ruler of the Synagogue not to be afraid nor worry because He had him covered! He had the situation under control. I am sure the Lord is still saying the same words to His children today, regardless of the circumstances that face us.

THE GREATEST ENEMY OF OUR FAITH IS FEAR

Let us look at another principle that made this extraordinary miracle possible. The scripture says:

> *And everyone who calls on the name of Lord will be saved. (Joel 2:32)*
> *But I called to God, and the Lord saved me (Psalms 55:16)*

These portions of scripture clearly reveal another principle that can be a great benefit for children of the living God. Note, that the ruler of the Synagogue went out of his own city to seek and call on the Lord for help. This is a very crucial principle and very important to cherish. The scripture says that "whosoever" shall call on the name of the Lord shall be saved. If the this ruler of the Synagogue called on the Lord and the Lord saved him, how much more shall He save His own children who call on Him? Child of God, you and I are precious in the sight of God and He will save us, regardless of the circumstances life may throw our way. If the Lord suspended His schedule and followed the ruler to his house because he came and called for Him, how much more will He follow His children in their deepest valley to save them from their troubles if they call on

Him? I tell you the gospel truth; you and I are more valuable, in the sight of God, because of the precious blood of Jesus Christ.

Therefore let us, with boldness, call on the name of the Lord both in season and out of season knowing that He will always be there for us. He can never disappoint us! We must develop ourselves in the word of God and allow the Holy Spirit to train us to refuse living in fearfulness because:

> *The one who is in you is greater than the one who is in the world. (1 John 4:4)*

The Bible makes three hundred and sixty five references to God Almighty telling His anointed children "Fear Not" neither be "Afraid." The number, three hundred and sixty five is a prophetic number because there are three hundred and sixty five days in a year. I believe that one of the significant reasons for this prophetic number is that the Lord wants His children to live without fear every day of the year.

The second significant reason the Lord wants His children to live without fear is because living a fearful life style has terrible and undesirable effects. Let us take a close look at the scripture message.

> *There is no fear in love; but perfect love casteth out fear: because fear hath torment. He that feareth is not made perfect in love. We love him, because he first loved us. (1John 4:18-19)*

The Lord wants His children to live a life full of love and not fear because fearfulness is a terrible bondage. It is filled with torment. Fear causes anxiety, high blood pressure, restlessness, sleeplessness, hopelessness, and destroys confidence just to mention a few. Needless to say, any of these types of torment can cause tragic and incurable sicknesses and diseases. We are created and sustained in Love. God is Love, He is our Father and we His children must live our lives full of love because perfect love casts out fear.

A third significant reason why He wants us to live fearlessly is because fear and faith can never work together as I pointed out earlier. A child of God who lives in fear fifty percent of the time and in faith fifty percent of the time would end up filled with nothing because fear and faith would cancel each other. Faith and fear are mortal enemies to one another. That is because they fight constantly seeking dominance. The one that dominates the person rules the entire life of that person.

The fourth reason why the Lord wants us to live in faith and not in fear is because our creator, the Almighty God cannot be pleased without faith.

YOUR FAITH PRODUCES A VICTORY REPORT AND MAKES GOD HAPPY

> *Now faith is the substance of things hoped for, the evidence of things not seen. For by it the elders obtained a good report.....But without faith it is impossible to please Him: for he that cometh to God must believe that He is, and that He is a rewarder of them that diligently seek Him.*
> *(Hebrews 11:1-2 and 6)*

It is obvious from this portion of the scripture and throughout the pages of the Bible that we cannot please God without faith. There is absolutely no room for negotiation with God in this subject. We, the children of the living God, washed with the blood of His dear Son either live and walk by faith and make Him happy or we live in fear and make Him unhappy. The choice is ours and not God's. In this chapter my goal, with the help of the Holy Spirit, is to equip and arm the church of Jesus Christ with tools from the word of God that will enable them to beginning living in faith and enjoying the benefits that come like never before. My dear friend, I want you to know that you don't have any business living in fear any more. The Bible says:

> *For God hath not given us the spirit of fear; but of power, and of love, and of sound mind. (2 Timothy 1:7)*

It is very important that you and I know who our enemy is because knowing your enemy helps you direct your God-given weapons effectively. The Devil and his forces are our enemies so let us direct our spiritual missiles against them, destroying them without fail. You and I must never forget what the love of God accomplished for us on the cross of Calvary. We have been justified by faith.

> *Therefore being justified by faith, we have peace with God through our Lord Jesus Christ. (Romans 5:1)*

Praise be to God because we are justified by our faith in the shed blood of Jesus Christ! Based on this scriptural fact, we, the children of God, are admonished by the scriptures to walk and live by faith every day of our lives.

> *For therein is the righteousness of God revealed from faith to faith: as it is*

written, the just shall live by faith.
(Romans 1:17)

In addition to the examples I use in this chapter to help us see how walking and living by faith did wonders in the lives of ordinary men and women in the Bible, the Lord has impressed on my spirit to use part of the chapter to develop, challenge, encourage and provoke us to a higher faith walk with God. Get ready, my friend, to step into a new dimension of faith walk with God.

It is very important to point out that your faith can never grow beyond your knowledge of God and His word. How can you have faith in a person whom you don't really know very well? Therefore, faith development Course 101 is that you begin to spend enough time in the word of God. The more you spend time with Him, the more the Holy Spirit will reveal Jesus Christ to you. If you know Jesus Christ well, you will automatically have knowledge of the living God. The scripture says:

For there are three that bear record in
heaven, the Father, the Word, and the
Holy Ghost: and these three are one.
(1 John 5:7)

I am very confident, by the authority of God's word, that as you study the word of God your knowledge of God will begin to enrich your life. The result of this process is that your faith will begin to develop and grow rapidly. Praise the Lord! If you are a new believer in the Lord, this is how the spiritual communication process works in the Kingdom of God. Whenever we go to God, with our needs in prayer, our heavenly Father listens to us. When we read the word of God, God Almighty speaks to us.

The more you read His Word, the Bible, the more God speaks to you and the more you listen to Him, His word will build up your faith. That is because:

> *So then faith cometh by hearing, and hearing by the word of God (Romans 10:17)*

Again, dear friend, my sincere prayer is that the revelation in this book will be a turning point in your life. The Lord says, regardless of circumstances you face right now, "Fear Not Only Believe" because GOD'S GOT YOU COVERED.

FEAR NOT GOD IS WITH YOU

One of the covenant promises God made with His children is His everlasting abiding presence with His children. It is the very nature of the living God to be with His children always. We can see this right from the beginning of creation, even in the Garden of Eden.

The Bible records:

> *And they heard the voice of the Lord God walking in the garden in the cool of the day: and Adam and his wife hid themselves from the presence of the Lord God amongst the trees of the garden. And the Lord God called unto Adam, and said unto him, where art thou?*
> *(Genesis 3:8-9)*

Here we clearly see that the Lord God Almighty has always taken great delight in being with his children. In the beginning of time God created the first man and woman and kept them in His presence, as I pointed out earlier in the book. The scripture says that God was in constant fellowship with Adam and Eve until that union was broken because of sin. But God sent a second Adam, Jesus Christ, into the world to restore you and me to God. All believers in the shed blood of His Son, on the cross of Calvary, live in God and God lives in them. It has always been the pleasure of the Lord to be with His children wherever they are. I want you to know that you are never alone, regardless of the circumstances that you face. I say to you, "Fear not, for the Lord God is with you." Because the Lord God is with us, you and I have no business living in fear, regardless of where we may be. As the sons and daughters of God we must have confidence that God's presence is always with us and that He is able to keep us from all the plans and attacks of the Devil and his forces. Let us look at some of these powerful promises of the living God in prayer that they will stir up your confidence in God.

> *Yea, though I walk through the valley of the shadow of death, I will fear no evil; for thou art with me. (Psalm 23:4)*
> *God has said, Never will I leave you; never will I forsake you. (Hebrews 13:5)*
> *So do not fear, for I am with you; do not be dismayed for I am your God. I will strength you and help you; I will uphold you with my righteous right hand. (Isaiah 41:10)*
> *Be strong and courageous. Do not be afraid or terrified because of them, for the Lord your God goes with you, he will never leave nor forsake you. (Deuteronomy 31:6)*
> *And surely I am with you always, to*

very end of the age. (Matthew 28:20)
The Lord himself goes before you and will be with you; he will never leave you nor forsake you. Do not be afraid; do not be discouraged.
(Deuteronomy 31:8)

These powerful promises are for you and me today. As He was with His children of old so He is with you and me. We can take God at His word; it will not fail. It is very important to know that we, as the children of God, can never see the glory and the wonder-working power of God unless we put our trust in His spoken words. I want you to know that our God is too big to lie. Therefore we can boldly take Him by His powerful promises that come out of His mouth.

My covenant will I not break, nor alter the thing that is gone out of my lips. (Psalm 89:34)
God is not a man, that he should lie, nor a son of man, that he should change his mind. Does he speak and then not act? Does he promise and not fufill? (Numbers 19:23)

We serve a living and powerful God. We can live our lives in confidence knowing that the Creator of the whole universe is with us always. Whatever we go through, the Lord has promised to be there with us even to the end of the world. When we take the Lord by His word He calms all fears that the Devil and his forces bring our way.

God Almighty is powerful and has everything it takes to keep His promises. How I pray that we will believe and put our trust in Him and watch Him manifest His glory to, through, and around us everyday.

> *When you pass through the waters, I will be with you; and when you pass through the rivers, they will not sweep over you. When you walk through the fire, the flame will not set you ablaze.* *(Isaiah 43:2)*

God's powerful promise has got us covered! Even when we go through the waters and fires of poverty, sickness, disease, pain, failure, hopelessness, and sleepless nights, God is always there with us to bring us through. His faithfulness endures forever and His unfailing power is always present with us. We can rest in His unchanging hands.

> *For I am the Lord, I change not; therefore ye sons of Jacob are not consumed. (Malachi 3:6)*

Child of God, you may be going through some troubled waters or flaming fires of life right this moment. You may not feel the touch of the Lord nor sense His presence. But, I want you to know that He is right in the middle of your trouble! He has promised never to leave you nor forsake you. The only reason He is there with you is to ensure your total safety. Always remember, that the bigger your troubles, the bigger our God becomes.

> *Where can I go trom your Spirit? Where can I flee from your presence? If I go up to the heavens, you are there; if I make my bed in the depth, you are*

there. If I rise on the wings of the dawn, if I settle on the far side of the sea, even there your hand will guide me, your right hand will hold me fast. If I say, Surely the darkness will hide me and the light become night around me, even the darkness will not be dark to you; the night will shine like the day, for darkness is as light to you. For you created my inmost being; you knit me together in my mother's womb.
(Psalm 139:7-13)

This portion of scripture and other portions throughout the pages of the Bible are clearly meant to exhort us to put our trust in the word of God. The Spirit of the Lord, by the hand of King David, is exhorting us that it really doesn't matter where we find ourselves and in whatever circumstances the Devil throws our way. The Lord has promised that He will never leave us nor forsake us. We can boldly stand tall in the face of the Devil and his forces and speak shaming words to them knowing that God has got us covered. If life circumstances force us down into the deepest pit, the Lord will be there with us. If we find ourselves on top of a mountain He will be there with us as well. We should rest on the promises of the Lord! Then and only then will we experience the wonderful presence of Him living in us. Always remember this fact, God will never disappoint you. You are the only one who can disappoint you.

The Lord is with you when you are with Him. If you seek Him, He will be found by you, but if you forsake Him, He will forsake you. (2 Chronicles 15:2)

The Spirit of the living God has given me utterance to bring these revelations to you. It is my sincere prayer that the Holy Ghost will open your eyes to understand so you can begin enjoying the powerful presence of God like never before. The precious promises of God are your covenant benefit as blood-bought followers of our Lord and Savior Jesus Christ. I pray that you catch the fire of these revelations. Begin to rest on the covenant promises of God. They are yours for the taking. They cannot fail because God cannot deny Himself. He and His words are inseparable, that is to say that God and His words are one.

Our God is trustworthy because He cannot fail. Why not take Him by His word and begin to experience the powerful presence of God manifested in your life today and forever. The scripture clearly says:

> God is our refuge and strength, an
> ever-present help in trouble.
> (Psalms 46:1)

Child of God, whatever you may be going through today, I encourage you to hang-in there because He has promised to be with you to the end.

THREE MEN WHO REFUSED TO BE AFRAID

This is the story of three men who made up their minds to defy a King's command, even in the face of death. They refused to be snared by fear and intimidation. I believe this true story will energize your faith to believe God for the breakthrough you desperately need today.

Let us look closely at what Almighty God did on

behalf of these three trusting men. What God did for them He can do for you, as well. All you need to do is stand your ground as they stood their ground, even in the face of death. God did not disappoint them neither will He disappoint you, if you put all your trust in Him. The Bible tells us:

> *Nebuchadnezzar the king made an image of gold, whose heights was threescore cubits, and the breadth thereof six cubits: he set it up in the plain of Dura, in the province of Babylon. Then Nebuchadnezzar the king sent to gather together the princes, governors, and the captains, and the judges, the treasurers, the counselors, the sheriffs, and all the rulers of the provinces, to come to the dedication of the image which Nebuchadnezzar the king had set up. Then the princes, governors, and captains, the judges, the treasurers, the counselors, the sheriffs, and all the rulers of the provinces, were gathered together unto the dedication of the image that Nebuchadnezzar the king had set up; and they stood before the image that Nebuchadnezzar had set up. Then an herald cried aloud, to you it is commanded, O people, nations, and languages. That at what time ye hear the sound of the cornet, flute, harp, sackbut, psaltery, dulcimer, and all kinds of musick, ye fall down and worship the golden image that Nebuchadnezzar the king hath set up. And whoso falleth not down and*

worshippeth shall the same hour be cast into the midst of a burning fiery furnace. Therefore at that time, when all the people heard the sound of the cornet, flute, harp, sackbut, psaltery, and all kinds of music, all the people, the nations, and languages, fell down and worshipped the golden image that Nebuchadnezzar the king had set up. Wherefore at that time certain Chaldeans came near, and accused the Jews. They spake and said unto the king Nebuchadnezzar, O king, live forever. Thou, O king, hast made a decree, that every man that shall hear the sound of the cornet, flute, harp, sackbut, psaltery, and dulcimer, and all kinds of music, shall fall down and worship the golden image. And whoso falleth not down and worshippeth, that he should be cast into the midst of a burning fiery furnace. There are certain Jews whom thou hast set over the affairs of the province of Babylon, Shadrach, Mechach, and Abednego, these men O king, have not regarded thee: they serve not thy gods, nor worship the golden image which thou hast set up. Then Nebuchadnezzar in his rage and fury commanded to bring Shadrach, Mechach, and Abednego. Then they brought these men before the king. Nebuchadnezzar spake and said unto them, is it true, O Shadrach, Mechach, and Abednego, do not ye serve my gods, nor worship the golden image which I have set up? Now if ye be ready that at what time ye hear the sound of the cornet, flute, harp, sackbut, psaltery, and dulcimer, and all kinds of music, ye fall down and worship the image which I have made; well: but if ye worship not, ye shall be cast the same hour into the midst of a burning fiery furnace; and who is that God that shall deliver you out of my hands? Shadrach, Mechach, and Abednego, answered and said to the king, O Nebuchadnezzar, we are not careful to answer thee in this matter. If it be so, our God whom we serve is able to deliver us from the burning fiery furnace, and he will deliver us out of thine hands, O king. But if not, be it known unto thee, O king, that we will not serve thy gods, nor worship the golden image which thou hast set up. Then was Nebuchadnezzar full of fury, and the form of his visage was changed against Shadrach, Mechach, and Abednego, therefore he spake, and commanded that they should heat the furnace more seven times more that it was wont to be heated. And he commanded the most mighty men that were in his army to bind Shadrach, Mechach, and Abednego, and to cast them into the burning fiery furnace. Then were these men bound in their coats, their hosen, and their hats, and their other garments, and were cast into the midst of the burning fiery furnace. Therefore because the king's commandment was urgent, and the *furnace exceedingly hot, the flame of the fire slew those men that took up Shadrach, Mechach, and Abednego. And these three men, Shadrach, Mechach, and Abedneo, fell down bound into the midst of the burning fiery furnace. Then Nebuchadnezzar the king was astonished, and rose up in haste, and spake, and said unto his counselors, Did we not cast three men bound into the midst of the fire? They answered and said unto the king, True, O king. He answered and said, Lo, I see four men loose, walking in the midst of the fire, and they have no hurt; and the form of the fourth is like the Son of God. Then Nebuchadnezzar came to the mouth of the burning fiery furnace, and spake, and said, Shadrach, Mechach, and Abednego, ye servants of the most high God, come forth, and come hither. Then Shadrach, Mechach, and Abednego, came forth of the midst of the fire. And the princes, governors, captains, and the king's counselors, being gathered together, saw these men, upon whose bodies the fire had no power, nor was an hair of their head singed, nor their coats changed, nor the smell of the fire passed on them. Then Nebuchdnezzar spake, and said, blessed be the God of Shadrach, Mechach, and Abednego, who hath sent his angel, and delivered his servants that trusted in him, and have changed the king's word, and yielded their bodies that they might not serve*

nor worship any god, except their own
God. Therefore I make a decree, That
every people, nation, and language,
which speak any thing amiss against
the God of Shadrach, Mechach, and
Abednego, shall be cut in pieces, and
their house shall be made a dunghill:
because there is no other God that can
deliver after this sort. Then the king
promoted Shadrach, Mechach, and
Abednego, in the province of Babylon.
(Daniel 3:1-30)

Child of God, this is an amazing encounter between the king and three young Jewish slaves in the land of Babylon. I have read this entire chapter many times. Every time I read it, my soul revives and is encouraged and kindled to a new level in my faith walk. I hope you have not forgotten that we are discussing the topic "Fear not, only believe." The story of these three young Jews fits our discussion, perfectly.

There are many faith-building lessons to be learned from this encounter. Let us address a few of them. It is my prayer that the Spirit of the living God will enlighten your understanding of the hidden treasures in this discussion.

The first spiritual lesson we must learn from this encounter is that these three young Jewish men were accused. Throughout the Bible, we find whenever a child of God purposes in his or her heart to pursue God and things of His Kingdom, the Devil and his agents arise with every thing they have to fight against them. The Bible says:

> *Wherefore at that time certain*
> *Chaldeans came near, and accused the*
> *Jews. (Daniel 3:8)*

And I heard a loud voice saying in heaven, Now is come salvation, and strength, and the Kingdom of our God, and the power of his Christ: for the accuser of the brethren is cast down, which accused them before our God day and night. (Revelation 12:10)

In the same way you must expect the Devil to accuse you because of your faith and stand with God. You must never be alarmed when it happens because God is watching over you and He has got you covered. The Devil is the accuser of the brethren!

The second lesson we learn from this encounter is that we must reaffirm our commitment and faith publicly or openly, regardless of the consequences. These three Jews without shame or fear reaffirmed their faith, commitment, and walk with God.

My dear friend, make no mistake about the fact that the Devil will do all he can, within his power, to tempt your stand and resolve. Steel is not created without passing through a fiery furnace! In the same way, our faith cannot be measured until it goes through testing by fire. The faith of these three men was tested and their first reaction was to openly reaffirm their faith, commitment, and walk with God. They answered and said to King Nebuchednezzar:

Shadrach, Mechach, and Abednego, answered and said to the king, O Nebuchadnezzar, we are not careful to answer thee in this matter. If it be so, our God whom we serve is able to deliver us from the burning fiery furnace, and he will deliver us out of thine hands, O king. But if not, be it known unto thee, O king, that we will

not serve thy gods, nor worship the
golden image which thou hast set up.
(Daniel 3:17-18)

Public affirmation of commitment, faith, and walk with God expels all fears and reinforces our confidence in unchanging God.

Thirdly, we must be prepared to die for what we believe, if need be. These men were prepared to die for what they believed and made it abundantly clear to the king that they were not going to serve his gods, regardless of the consequences.

> *And he said to them all, if any man will*
> *come after me, let him deny himself,*
> *and take up his cross daily and follow*
> *me. For whosoever shall save his life*
> *shall lose: and whosoever shall lose his*
> *life for my sake, the same shall save it.*
> *(Luke 9:23-24)*

The fourth lesson we must learn from this encounter is that you must in the midst of your trouble expect God to show up. They were firm and unshaken by the threat of the king even so must we be firm in our commitment to the Lord and Savior of our lives. These men of faith believed that God was very much able to deliver them from the burning furnace and from the hands of the king. You need not worry about your safety for the Lord will show up, right on time, to deliver you from the hands of your enemies. You can count on Him!

> *Then Nebuchadnezzar the king was*
> *astonished, and rose up in haste, and*
> *spake, and said unto his counselors,*

"Did not we cast three men bound into the midst of the fire?" They answered and said unto the king, "True, O king." He answered and said, "Lo, I see four men loose, walking in the midst of the fire, and they have no hurt; and the form of the fourth is like the Son of God. (Daniel 3:24-25)

God is our refuge and strength, a very present help in trouble. (Psalm 46:1)

When thou passest through the waters, I will be with thee; and through the rivers, they shall not over flow thee: when thou walkest through the fire, thou shall not be burned: neither shall the flame kindle upon thee. (Isaiah 43:2)

Therefore because the king's commandment was urgent; and the flame exceedingly hot, the flame of the fire slew those men that took up Shadrach, Mechach, and Abednego. (Daniel 3:21)

The fifth lesson that we learn from this encounter is that the Lord will handle our enemies for us. We see from this encounter that there is promotion after a time of testing is completed. The young Jewish slaves were promoted after their testing was completed. If we hang in there during the testing period, which all of us have to go through to test our commitment and faith in the Lord, there is no doubt that our promotion will come.

Then the king promoted Shadrach, Mechach, and Abednego, in the province of Babylon. (Daniel 3:30)

A TRUE TESTIMONY

In a certain elementary school, there was a six-year old boy who had been taught about God by his single-parent mother. His mother had always taught him that God would always be there for him, even in troubled or difficult times. The season came for the elementary school's spelling bee contest. The young boy miraculously made it through the preliminary phase and into the final elimination. As God planned it, the young boy was one of two finalists left to compete for the trophy. On the last day of competition, the boy and his competitor stood before the entire school audience and hundreds of people from the community. Before the competition began, the young boy remembered what his mother had taught him, that God would always be there for him.

When it came time to spell the last word the conductor of the competition asked them to spell "refrigeration." The other student missed it and left it to the young church boy to spell it correctly. The trophy would be his to carry home. The young boy bowed his head to the ground and whispered, "Lord, you promised to be with me in times of trouble. Now is the time, Lord, save me from this trouble." He looked out the window and there he saw a delivery van pulling into the school premises to deliver some electronic equipment to the school office. On the side of the van he saw, REFRIGERATION EQUIPMENT. The young boy quickly spelled refrigeration correctly and became the champion of the school.

Child of God, it is amazing what our God can do for His children. In this true testimony, we see that at the very time the young boy seemed to be in trouble, the Lord sent an electronic appliance truck by a window where the young boy could see it. Praise be to the name of the Lord, Amen. I shared this testimony to build up your faith in the Lord. He will not fail you. He will always be there for you, even in difficult and challenging times.

Chapter 10

NEVER QUIT TRUSTING GOD

Though He slay me, yet will I trust in Him: but I will maintain mine own ways before Him" (Job 13:15)

My dear friend, as I pointed out earlier in the book, it may be encouraging for you to know that throughout the pages of the Bible, there is no single place where the Lord promised His children a "trouble or battle free life," but He did assuredly guarantee us a "defeat-free life." There is overwhelming evidence supporting the fact that every child of God, at one point or another in their lives, must go through some testing. Yes, you heard me correctly! Every child of God must go through a time of testing. I hope this statement does not shock you. If you have not gone through a time of testing or trial of your faith since you became born again you better get ready! It shall surely come and it may not be too long from now. Our biblical characters such as Abraham, Joseph, King David, Ruth, Esther, Elijah, Moses, the disciples and our Lord Jesus Christ just to mention a few were all tested. The Bible tells us that:

Man that is born of a woman is of a few days, and full of trouble. (Job 14:1)

It is a fact that after the fall of mankind and because of the disobedience and sin of Adam and Eve in the Garden of Eden, perils, trouble, and problematic times came into the human race. The scriptures and our every day experiences prove to us that life is a long journey and our days are spent in constant battles. In the Bible, we find events to support the fact that those who made vigorous effort to live a godly life were attacked by the Devil and his agents. The Bible tells us:

> Persecutions, afflictions, which came upon me at Antioch, at Iconium, at Lystra; what persecution I endured: but out of them all the Lord delivered me. Yea, and all that will live godly in Christ Jesus shall suffer persecution.
> (2 Timothy 3:11-12)
> Many are the afflictions of the righteous: but the Lord delivereth him out of them all. He keepeth all his bones: not one of them is broken. (Psalms 34:19-20)

Based on these portions of scripture, the Apostle Paul and King David emphatically remind us that our righteous walk and holy relationship with God will attract the kingdom of darkness against our lives. My personal walk and relationship with the Lord, coupled with my every day experiences, prove to me that at the very instant we purpose and set our heart to pursue God all the forces of hell will be loosed against us to prevent us from living a life that is pleasing to God. The above portions of scripture and the revelation that I am about to share with you came to me by the hands of the Holy Spirit.

YOUR FAITH WILL BE TESTED BY FIRE

In this chapter, we are going to look closely into the lives of two individuals who were no strangers to persecution, trials, afflictions, and constant battles in life because of their relationship with the living God. Both of these individuals exhort and encourage us through their writings to stand firm in the Lord knowing that in all of our trials and tribulations He who has called us will not fail to deliver us. Therefore, in rough and difficult times, we must never cease to put our trust in the living God!

The book of Job is one of the oldest books in the whole Bible and out of it comes one of the greatest lessons we can ever learn. As God's children we can firmly put our "trust" in the living God, especially in difficult and testing times. The Bible tells us:

> There was a man in the land of Uz, whose name was Job; and that man was perfect and upright, and one that feared God, and eschewed evil. And there were born unto him seven sons and three daughters. His substance also was seven thousand sheep, and three thousand camels, and five hundred yoke of oxen, and five hundred she asses, and a very great household; so that this man was the greatest of all the men of the east. (Job 1:1-3)

Job was not only a righteous man but also a man who loved God with all of his heart. He was an upright, God fearing man who was perfect in the sight of man and God. According to the Bible, God blessed the work of Job's hands and gave him a great household. Everything was going well for him and he could not have asked for anything more. He was a prosperous man and very wealthy. As a result of Job's walk and relationship with God, coupled with the blessings of God upon his life, Satan began to focus on him. He became jealous of Job and set his eyes on him. The Bible tells us the following:

> *Now there was a day when the sons of God came to present themselves before the Lord, and Satan came also among them. And the Lord said unto Satan, whence comest thou? Then Satan answered the Lord, and said, From going to and fro in the earth, and from walking up and down in it. And the Lord said unto Satan, Hast thou considered my servant Job, that there is none like him in the earth, a perfect and upright man, one that feareth God, and escheweth evil. Then Satan answered the Lord, and said, Doth Job fear God for nought? Hast thou not made an hedge about him, and about his house, and about all that he hath on every side? Thou hast blessed the works of his hands, and his substance is increased in the land. But put forth thine hands now, and touch all that he hath, and he will curse thee to thy face. (Job 1:6-11)*

There are some valuable lessons in this book of Job that I believe greatly benefit us in our walk and relationship with our heavenly Father. First, biblically, it is no secret and should not be shocking to any child of God to know that at the very moment we make a commitment to live a righteous and upright life the Devil and his wicked forces are on our trails. In the above dialog between the living God and Satan, the Devil recognized that he could not touch Job, his household, and everything that pertained to him because God had placed a hedge of protection around them.

Second, we see from the dialog that God bragged of the righteousness and upright life style of Job and boasted, without reservation, that regardless of what Job would go through he would never curse Him to His face as Satan had predicted. God had faith in Job and boasted that regardless of any circumstances life might bring to his path that Job would never cease to follow Him.

Third, the Lord made it abundantly clear to Satan that Job's righteousness and uprightness of heart was not dependent on the blessings he had received. These are crucial lessons that we should mediate upon daily. God the Father counted Job worthy to stand his ground regardless of the deceptive attacks the Devil would make against his life.

My dear friend, can God count on you to do His will? According to the Bible, after the dialog between the Lord and Satan ended, the Lord allowed Satan to go ahead and tempt Job. We find from Job's account that shortly after the talk between the Lord and Satan ended, the Devil attacked Job like a mad dog and went violently against him from all angles.

First, the Devil went after the family of Job and crushed them with death and destruction. Job lost his ten children within a short period of time. In other words, Job attended ten funeral services of his children in a day. The calamity for Job did not end there. According to the Bible, Job's great wealth and possessions were attacked and destroyed. Specifically, his flocks were destroyed and eliminated. Everything that Job had went down the drain in a very short period of time. The Devil was on a destructive rampage against Job and everything in his life. Yet, Job stood strong and continued his unshakeable attitude of worship and thanksgiving to God. The Bible tells us that after the Devil killed all the children of Job and destroyed his livelihood, he went ahead and attacked his body with sickness and disease.

Child of God, remember the mission of the Devil is to steal, kill, and destroy. This was exactly what he did to Job and make no mistake about it, that is what he wants to do to you and me. There is no question about it, the Devil's eyes are upon you by virtue of the fact that you are a child of the living God. Thanks be to God! The blood of our Lord Jesus Christ has redeemed us from the wicked devices and strategies of the Devil. We have power over him and his forces through the powerful name of the Lord Jesus Christ! Therefore as in the case of Job, we must strive not to give in to the bastard Devil and his wicked strategic devices. We know this fact very well: The Lord is always with us to ensure that we live victoriously over the Devil and his forces.

> *So went Satan forth from the presence of the Lord, and smote Job with sore boils from the sole of his feet to unto his crown.(Job 2:7)*

Job went through a difficult and perilous period of his life. The Bible records that his physical condition was so deplorable that his wife and his friends suggested ceaselessly that he should curse God and die. But Job refused to do so.

> *Then said his wife unto him, Dost thou still retain thine integrity? Curse God*

*and die. Bit he said unto her, thou
speakest as one of the foolish women
speaketh. Shall we receive good at the
hand of God, and shall we not receive
evil? In all this did not Job sin with his
lips. Now when Job's three friends
heard of all this evil that was come
upon him, they came every one from
his own place; Eliphaz the Temanite,
and Bildad the Shuhite, and Zophar the
Naamathite: for they had made an
appointment together to come to mourn
with him and to comfort him. And when
they lifted up their eyes afar off, and
knew him not, they lifted their voice,
and wept; and they rent every one their
mantle, and sprinkled dust upon their
heads towards heaven. So they sat
down with him upon the ground seven
days and seven nights, and none spake
a word unto him: for they saw that his
grief was very great. (Job 2:9-13)*

In the above portion of scripture we find that Job
was very determined and courageous. He would not
curse God to His face in spite of tragedies that he
suffered and his undesirable physical conditions, as
Satan had anticipated and predicted.

Child of God, it should not be shocking for you to
know that life is a long journey and filled with troubles
and challenges. As I mentioned earlier in the book, it
is incorrect to assume that our lives will be battle-free
simply because we have a relationship and walk with
God. That is simply not the case! In fact, the
beginning of our relationship and walk with God,
through our Lord and Savior Jesus Christ, signals the
beginning of lifelong battle with the Devil and his

forces. As we journey through life, we must be fully prepared and armed with the Word of God to fight against him especially in the difficult and challenging times of our lives.

Since the fall of mankind, in the Garden of Eden, each one of us will at one point or another go through a storm in life. The good news is that storms are periodical! Therefore, whatever circumstances or challenges you go through you should be strong and courageous. Put your trust in the Lord for He has promised that He will "never leave you nor forsake you." (Hebrews 13:5)

Another unbiblical misconception that most of us make, especially new believers in Christ, is that all our trials, testing, and troubles are as a result of sin and disobedience to God. But that is an incomplete truth. The trouble that Job went through shows us that our every-day battles of life may not be only because of our sin or disobedience to God. According to the Bible, Job's ordeal was not as a result of his misdeeds but because the Devil is an enemy of the good works of God.

A second incorrect assumption that most believers make is that the troubles we have in life is God's way of teaching his children lessons. The assumption may be partially true. As a loving Father, God sometimes, with love, allows His children to go through some troubles. In the case of Job, we can see that his trouble was not as a result of any sin or disobedience but simply because the Devil was jealous of Job's relationship with God. Job was very determined not to let the Lord down, even in the face of intense pressure from his wife and friends.

Another person who was no stranger to tribulations, trials, and troubles because of his dedicated walk and relationship with God through the Lord Jesus Christ was the Apostle Paul. In one of his writings, he stated the following,

> *We are troubled on every side, yet not distressed; we are perplexed, but not in despair; Persecuted, but not forsaken; cast down, but not destroyed; Always bearing about in the body the dying of the Lord Jesus, that the life also of Jesus might be made manifest in our body. For we which are alive are always delivered unto death for Jesus' sake, that the life also of Jesus might be made manifest in our mortal body. (1 Corinthians 4:8-11)*

We can sense and feel the intensity of pain from the tone of Apostle Paul's writing. I sense in my spirit that this period of his writing was a very difficult time for him. The Bible records how Paul was beaten many times and left on the road to die. He was in prison numerous times and suffered many things for the Gospel's sake. Yet he kept on going.

My dear friend, at one point or another in our lives we are bound to go through a time of testing and tribulation. It is not a question of whether our faith will be tested but when our faith will be tested. If our faith and integrity in the Lord is not tried and tested, as gold is tried and tested in a furnace of fire, we will never know what we are made of. In the time of testing it is refreshing to know that *"the Lord will not allow us to be tempted beyond what we can bear or handle." (1 Corinthians 10:13)* In trying times, we must put our trust in the Lord knowing that "He is with us all the way" even In the midst our troubles.

BE ON GUARD SATAN WILL ATTACK YOU AT YOUR WEAKEST POINT

There is no question about it, Satan will attack you when you are down and out. We must be on the lookout for points in our lives when our back is against the wall. It is then Satan goes on the rampage.

Satan attacked Job on every side but he kept his eyes on the Lord. God had confidence in him. He knew that Job would never let Him down as Satan had boasted and predicted. The Devil used Job's wife and his three friends to tempt him, at his weakest point, when they suggested to him that he should curse God and die. The secret here is that the Devil never attacks us at out strongest point but at our weakest and most venerable. In fact, he tempted our Savior, Jesus Christ, after He had fasted for forty days and forty nights in the wilderness. Therefore, in trying times we must never cease to put our trust in the Lord knowing that God has got us covered. The Bible records:

> *Many are the afflictions of the righteous but the Lord delivereth him from them all. He keepeth his bones and none of them is broken. (Psalms 34:19-20)*

When we find ourselves faced with challenges and the troubles of life, we must believe that God will not fail to deliver us. The Bible tells us:

IN TOUGH TIMES, NEVER TAKE YOUR EYES AWAY FROM THE LORD

And straightway Jesus constrained his

disciples to get into the ship, and to go before Him unto the other side, while he sent the multitudes away. And when he had sent the multitudes away, he went up into a mountain apart to pray: and when the evening was come, he was there alone. But the ship is now in the midst of the sea, tossed with waves: for the wind was contrary. And in the fourth watch of the night Jesus went unto them, walking on the sea. And when the disciples saw him walking on the sea, they were troubled, saying, it was a spirit; and they cried out for fear. But straightway Jesus spake unto them, saying, "Be of good cheer; it is I; be not afraid." And Peter answered him and said, "Lord, if it be thou, bid me come unto thee on the water." And he said, "Come." And when Peter was come down out of the ship, he walked on the water, to go to Jesus. But when he saw the wind was boisterous, he was afraid; and beginning to sink, he cried, saying, "Lord, save me." And immediately Jesus stretched forth his hand, and caught him and said unto him, "O thou of little faith, wherefore didst thou doubt?" (Matthew 14:22-31)

Our key to victory, especially when our backs are against the wall, is to keep our eyes on the Lord. It is obvious that Satan will do everything within his power to distract us. To ensure our total victory we must be on our guard. Keep your eyes on the Lord!

In the above event, the Bible tells us that after the Lord miraculously fed a great multitude of people, with five loaves of bread and two fishes, he commanded His disciples to get into a ship and head to the other side of the sea while He sent the people away. When the ship got to the middle of the sea, it was rocked by furious waves and the lives of the disciples were in great danger. While this was happening, the Lord was alone on a mountain, praying. When He realized the disciples were in jeopardy He went to meet them. The scripture tells us when the disciples saw someone walking on the sea they became terrified. Not knowing that it was the Lord they cried out. Then the Lord told them that it was He and they should not be afraid. To make sure it was the Lord, Peter asked to come to him on the water. The Lord invited him to do so. Peter set out, walking on the water, towards the Lord. But when he saw the fury of the waves he took his eyes off the Lord and began to sink. He cried out and the Lord saved him.

The valuable lesson for us here is that in troubles and difficult times we must not take our focused eyes off the Lord. If we are down, our way upward is to call on the name of the Lord. He saved Job and Peter when they called on Him, He will assuredly save us if we call on Him, even in the midst of great danger.

> For I know that my redeemer liveth, and that He shall stand at the latter day upon the earth. (Job 19:25)
> For I know in whom I have believed. (2Timothy 1:12)

As children of the living God we must confidently put our trust in the Lord, knowing that He has the power to keep and deliver us, regardless of what we may face in life each day. The Bible tells us that God restored all that the Devil and his forces of darkness had stolen from Job. Whatever the Devil may have stolen from you, the scriptures guarantee that the Lord will restore it to you.

> *The Lord turned the captivity of Job, when he prayed for his friends: also the Lord gave Job twice as much as he had before. (Job 42:10)*

Our God is still in the restoration business. What He did for Job He will do for you. All we need to do is put our eyes on Him, focus and trust even in the face of seemingly insurmountable circumstances. *"There is nothing too hard for Him." (Jeremiah 32:27)*

There are more valuable lessons to be learned from the troubles that came upon Job. First, we saw that Satan was originally not able to touch Job, his family, and all that God had given to him because God had his protective hedge around him, his family, and his possessions. We should trust and be confident that He has the same protective hedge around us. The scripture tells us that:

> *As the mountains are round about Jerusalem, so the Lord is round about His people from henceforth and for ever. (Psalms 125:2)*

The same God that protected Job is also our protector. He is still on the throne, alive and well.

Second, we see, through Job's time of troubles, that regardless of our troubles and tribulations "The Lord will never leave nor forsake us." The scripture tells us that:

> *Because he hath set his love upon me, therefore will I deliver him: I will set him*

on high, because he hath known my name. He shall call upon me, and I will answer him: I will be with him in trouble; I will deliver him, and honor him. With long life will I satisfy him and shew him my salvation. (Psalms 91:14-16)

As the Lord was with Job even so He is with us today. He is with us to deliver us from our troubles! All we need do to ensure our total victory is put all of our trust in God, like Job.

The third lesson we learn from Job is that *"The Lord turned the captivity of Job when he prayed for his friends." (Job 42:10)* This is very important because it reminds us to discipline ourselves to pray for the salvation and forgiveness of those whose plans are aimed at discouraging us from doing God's perfect "will" in our lives. We saw when Job began to pray for his friends who suggested that "he should curse God and die" God rescued him from his troubles and rewarded him with a double portion of all that he had lost. God will restore everything that the enemy has stolen from his children. Therefore, "let us be strong in the Lord and in the power of His might" (Ephesians 6:10-12) knowing that the battles of our lives are God's battles and not our own. If Job could make it you and I can also make it! So, in trying times, never quit trusting the Lord because He has got you covered.

The good news is that whatever you may be going through today, you will come through it because God has got you covered. It may seem and feel like you are not coming out of your current circumstances but the Devil is lying to you. You are coming out of them, triumphantly. Hold your peace, stand still and God will bring you out of your troubles. Never forget that God has got you covered!

Chapter 11

DOCTORS DON'T HAVE THE LAST WORD

Who his own self bare our sins in his own body on the tree, that we, being dead to sins, should live unto righteousness: by whose stripes ye were healed. (1 Peter 2:24)
He sent His word, and healed them, and delivered them from their destructions. (Psalm 107:20)
For I am the Lord that healeth thee. (Exodus 15:26)

In the Bible we find countless verses confirming and supporting the fact that it is the perfect "will" of God for His children to live in divine health. In fact, before the fall of the first man and woman, Adam and Eve, there was no sickness or disease on the planet earth. Hence they lived and dwelt in a perfect state of health. But when Adam and Eve disobeyed the command of the living God they sinned against Him. Then sickness and disease came into the human race as a result of sin. In order to redeem the human race from the dominion of sin, sickness and disease, the living God sent His only Son, the Lord Jesus

Christ. He came into the world to pay the ultimate price for sin so that, through His sacrificial blood, He would destroy the power of sickness and disease over us. Through the blood covenant of Jesus we obtain our physical healing and also maintain and retain our health. Let me emphatically state again, based upon the promises of the living God, it is the perfect "will" of God for His children to live in divine health.

Child of God, you may be faced with physical illness, right at this moment. Your doctor may have given you a terrible report regarding your health. He may have told you that you are not going to make it. But, I have good news for you. The Devil is a liar and the father of all lies! Your doctor does not have the final say, God does! You can make it! The precious blood of the Lord Jesus Christ has already paid for your healing. It is a done deal! All you need to do is exercise your faith, backed by the word of God, to obtain the healing that is rightfully yours. It is the powerful word of God that carries anointing to manifest the healing you desperately need today.

Many people ask me "Why is it that miraculous physical healing is not happening today as it was in the Apostle's days?" The answer is simple! First, It is because many people put their trust in their doctors, medicine, and the government's health system more than they do in God when they are sick. Hence many people fail to believe and trust God enough for physical healing. Many also fail to obtain healing because they do not put their faith to work and act upon the words of God. My mission in this chapter is to communicate the good news of God's word to help build up your faith. This will enable you to believe God for physical healing that you desperately need.

PHYSICAL HEALING BELONGS TO YOU

My dear friend, physical healing belongs to you because you are under the new covenant, made on your behalf, by the sacrificially shed blood of the Lord Jesus Christ. So, regardless of the challenges or nature of your physical condition and regardless of the bad news your doctor may have told you, your doctor does not have the last word concerning your life. God does. It is only what God has to say that really matters! The Bible emphatically tells us:

> *There are many devices in a man's heart; nevertheless the counsel of the Lord, that shall stand. (Proverbs 19:21)*

One of the amazing works God did for us on the Cross of Calvary was the redemption of mankind from sin and it's consequences. The work of redemption was completed when the Lord Jesus Christ, the only Son of God, gave His life for the remission of our sins. When the Lord was placed on the Cross and died for us, sin and all its consequences were also nailed to that Cross. Through our faith in the sacrificial blood we can boldly proclaim, "we are redeemed from sin and all the works of sin." It is very important that we know the extent of our redemption. The Bible tells us:

> *That Christ hath redeemed us from the curse of the law, being made a curse for us: for it is written, cursed is every one that hangeth on a tree.*
> *(Galatians 3:13)*

When Jesus destroyed the power of sin at Calvary, He also destroyed sickness and disease on our behalf. In order for us to really appreciate His redemptive work, I would encourage you to carefully read and study the book of Deuteronomy, the twenty-eighth chapter, beginning from verse fifteen through to the end. From this portion of scripture we find that the Lord Jesus Christ, through His precious sacrificial covenant blood, not only paid for our sins but also paid for our sickness and disease. Ironically, many children of God have difficulty believing that their sicknesses and disease have been paid for on the Cross of Calvary.

In this book and specifically in this chapter, I have made the point that to receive healing it is very important that you have a personal walk and relationship with God. In other words, that you are a born- again child of God. This is very important to ensure the full benefit of the new covenant blessings and full manifestation of God's promises will come alive as you read through the pages of this book. The redemptive blood of the Lord Jesus Christ has paid the ultimate price for our sins and also for our physical healing. King David recorded in one of his writings the following for our exhortation.

> *Bless the Lord, O my soul: and all that is within me, bless His holy name. Bless the Lord, O my soul, and forget not all His benefits. Who forgiveth all thine iniquities; who healeth all thine diseases. (Psalms 103:1-3)*

King David discovered, in his days, that it was the Lord that forgave his iniquities and healed his diseases. The atoning blood of the Lord Jesus Christ purchased physical healing for us. It is a done deal! It does not matter whether our body feels like it or not, the Lamb of God paid for our healing when He died on the Cross of Calvary. In this chapter my mission is to teach you how to appropriate healing by faith. It is your faith in the incorruptible Word of God that will make you whole! It is your faith in the living Word of God that brings the healing that you desperately need, regardless of the nature of the illness and disease afflicting your body. You can have your health back in the name of Jesus and by His atoned sacrificial blood.

ONLY YOUR FAITH CAN MAKE YOU WHOLE

Why is faith vital to appropriate physical healing? Because the Bible tells us:

> Now faith is the substance of things hoped for, the evidence of things not seen. For by it the elders obtain a good report. But without faith it is impossible to please Him: for He that cometh to God must believe that He is, and that He a rewarder of them that diligently seek Him. (Hebrews 11:1-2, 6)

Faith is the vehicle through which God's children obtain anything from Him including physical healing. Faith is very crucial to our walk and relationship with God. Make no mistake about it, we can receive nothing from God the Father without it! By faith we believe in God the Father, Son, and the Holy Ghost. By faith we obtain our salvation, through the blood of Jesus Christ. Everything we are and have is as a result of our faith in God. We also believe that when our journey here is over we will spend eternity with God; that is an act of faith. No wonder the Apostle Paul wrote these words *"The just shall live by*

179

faith" (Romans 1:17).

In like manner, we must put our faith to work to obtain physical healing. Therefore whatsoever we need from our heavenly Father, including healing for our physical body, we must ask and receive it by faith. Child of God, there is no other way around it! It is our faith in the living Word of God that invites the hands of God to perform mighty miracles in our lives.

There are many biblical methods that God uses to administer physical healing to His children. In this chapter, I want to speak on one of these methods and share with you seven key steps to physical healing. First, the Bible tells us:

> And it shall come to pass, that whosoever shall call on the name of the Lord shall be delivered. (Joel 2:32)

One of the benefits we have as children of God is that we serve a living God. He is alive and not dead! We serve a God who answers prayers and we can count on Him to answer us whenever we wholeheartedly call upon His name. The Word of God guarantees us that God will deliver us from all of our troubles if we dare to call upon His name. Ironically many children of God fail to take God by His word to call on His name when they are in trouble and most often they attempt to call on the Lord after they have exhausted all other options. This ought not to be so! The throne room of God should be the first stop in calling for help for every child of God. It is very important that we call on the Lord, especially in troubled times, because it shows that we have faith in the rescuing hands of unchangeable God to deliver us.

Chapter 12

SEVEN KEYS TO PHYSICAL HEALING

The seven key steps to physical healing I am about to share with you have the authority of the Word of God. They are capable of turning your unbelief into faith to help you believe God for physical healing. All that you need to appropriate your physical healing is faith in the living Word of God. The Bible tells us:

> *Is any sick among you? Let him call for the elders of the church: and let them pray over him, anointing him with oil in the name of the Lord. And the pray of faith shall save the sick, and the lord shall raise him up; and if he have committed sins, they shall be forgiven him. Confess your fault one to another, and prayer for one another, that ye may be healed. The effectual fervent prayer of a righteous man availeth much. (James 5:14-16)*

We find, from the above portion of scripture, the prescribed method laid down by the Spirit of God for

181

believers to appropriate faith and receive physical healing. It is very crucial that we understand that the healing method applies to believers only and not to everyone.   In other words, the physical healing method prescribed above applies only to those who have been washed with the sacrificial blood of the Son of God and have accepted the Lord Jesus Christ as their personal Lord and Savior.

CALL FOR THE ELDERS OF THE CHURCH

The first step to physical healing for believers, as prescribed by the Spirit of the Lord in [James 5:14-16], is that the sick or afflicted believer should call for the Elders of the Church. The Bible tells us that if a child of God is overtaken by sickness or disease he or she should do this because the Elders of the Church are the delegated authority of God for the Church of Jesus Christ.   The Elders are the spokesmen and women of God and also overseers of the Church. Also, the Lord wants us to call for them when we are overtaken by sickness or disease because they are the vessels through which the Lord channels His blessings into the lives of His children. .

It is historically true that every tragedy is a result of ignored instructions. Therefore, if we want to experience the full manifestation of the power and glory of God in our lives, we must follow the instructions the Spirit of God has laid out for our physical healing.   It is the perfect "will" of our heavenly Father for us to live in divine health. Should we be overtaken by sickness or disease, the Lord want us to call for the Elders of the Church so they can pray for our complete physical healing and restoration. Healing is the right for every believer and not just a privilege.

THE ELDERS OF THE CHURCH MUST PRAY FOR THE SICK PERSON

The second key step for physical healing and total restoration is that the Elders of the Church should pray a prayer of faith over the afflicted person. This second step is very crucial because without a faith-based prayer of agreement, between the sick believer and the Elders of the Church, there will be no miracle healing manifestation. The Bible asks us:

Can two walk together, except they be agreed? (Amos 3:3)

The Lord delegates His power to the Elders of the Church activating His healing power for the believer but the sick believer must be in agreement when they pray over him or her to make it happen..

Many believers fail to receive physical healing not because God does not love them or want to heal them but because of their unbelief and hardness of heart. I have seen many Christians attend healing crusades and see sick persons on their right or left side miraculously healed and completely restored. Yet you can hear him or her praying "Lord if it be your will, heal me." Why was this person not healed as the other folks were? Because of unbelief and lack of knowledge of the Word, period! Our God is no respecter of persons. If He heals one person He will heal anybody. Let us claim the word of God and conquer that wicked spirit of unbelief in our lives!

We can then begin to enjoy the fullness of all the blessings of God, including physical healing and total restoration of our body. Therefore, it is very crucial that the sick and afflicted believer be in harmony and total agreement with the Elders of the Church when he or she is being prayed for concerning complete physical healing and restoration. The Bible also tells us:

> *Verily I say unto you, whatsoever ye shall bind on earth shall be bound in heaven: and whatsoever ye shall loose on earth shall be loosed in heaven, Again I say unto you, That if two of you shall agree on earth as touching any thing that they shall ask, it shall be done for them of my Father which is in heaven. (Matthew 18:18-19)*

The Lord will perform what He has promised to do, but are we willing to do what He has instructed us to do?

THE SICK PERSON MUST BE ANOINTED WITH A CONSECRATED OIL

The third key step for the believer's physical healing and total restoration is that the Elders of the Church must anoint the sick folk with oil, in the name of the Lord. For the interest of new believers, the "anointing oil" symbolizes the mighty Spirit of God bestowed upon the individual being anointed. In the Old Testament, the Prophets used anointing oil to dedicate and consecrate those chosen by God. When they were anointed the mighty Spirit of God descended upon the person. The Bible tells us,

> *The Samuel took the horn of oil, and anointed him in the midst of his brethren: And the Spirit of the LORD came upon David from that day forward. So Samuel rose up, and went to Ramah. (1Samuel 16:13)*

184

This is an important step because the Bible records that "It is the anointing that destroys the yoke" (Isaiah 10:27). Again, if a child of God is overtaken with illness or disease, the Bible precisely instructs that he or she should call for the Elders of the Church, the Elders should pray over the sick or afflicted believer in conjunction with anointing them with oil.

THE PRAYER OF FAITH
PRODUCES HEALING

The fourth key step for the believer's physical healing is that the Elders of the Church must pray a prayer of faith for the sick or afflicted believer. As pointed out earlier, a prayer of faith is very crucial because it is our faith that moves the hands of God to perform wonders in the lives of His children. The prayer of Faith is the prayer that agrees with the promises of God that God has the power and ability to perform and do exactly what He has promised to do. The Bible tells us that when we pray and ask anything from God we should ask it in faith.

> But let Him ask in faith, nothing waving.
> For he that wavereth is like a wave of
> the sea driven with the wind and
> tossed. For let not that man think that
> he shall receive any thing of the Lord.
> (James 1:6-7)

Therefore, when the Elders pray for the sick and afflicted believers, the Elders must pray in confidence and faith knowing that God is able to do what He has promised to do, that is to heal them. To help the Elders of the Church pray for the sick and afflicted with faith, boldness, and in confidence, the Elders must locate the healing scriptures [the promises of God] to support their faith and confidence. The following are my favorite healing scriptures:

> *And this is the confidence that we have in him, that if we ask any thing according to his will, he heareth us. And if we know that he hears us, whatsoever we ask, we know that we have the petitions that we desired of him.*
> *John 5:14-15)*
> *He sent his word and healed them and delivered them from their destruction.*
> *(Psalm 107:20)*
> *Now faith is the substance of things hoped for, the evidence of things not seen. For by it the elders obtained a good report. But without faith it is impossible to please him, for he that cometh to God must believe that he is, and that he is the rewarder of them that diligently seek him.*
> *(Hebrews 11: 1-2, 6)*

Therefore, when I pray for the sick and afflicted, I pray in faith and confidence because I know it is God's perfect "will" for His children to be in divine health. We should always abide in faith knowing that the Word of God cannot fail.

THE SICK PERSON MUST CONFESS HIS OR HER SINS TO GOD

The fifth key step to the sick believer's physical healing and total restoration is that the believer must confess his or her sins and faults to God and ask Him for forgiveness. The sick and afflicted person must also confess their faults to the Elders of the Church, in confidence. This is biblically right, in the sight of God! Recently a young, newly married woman called our Victory Prayer Line after she watched our daily television program "Hour of Restoration" in Minnesota. I returned her call and asked what she wanted us to pray for. She said to me, "I need to ask God's forgiveness for cheating on my husband." I humbly rebuked her, with love, and counseled her to repent. Sometimes, we need to confess our faults to those whom we trust, especially our spiritual leaders, so they can earnestly pray with us and help us work through our weaknesses and guide us back on the path of righteousness. What this fifth key step really says is that the sick individual should not be ashamed to tell fellow believers, whom they trust and in whom they have confidence, the difficulties they may be going through so that prevailing prayers can be made for them. The Bible tells us that we are "our brother's keeper." This means that we share our struggles with one another and bear one another's burdens by praying for healing.

THE LORD WILL HEAL THE SICK

Sixth, after we obediently follow the pathway to healing instructions stipulated in [James 5:14-16], the Lord will heal the sick.

> *My covenant will I not break, nor alter the things that is gone out of my lips. (Psalms 89:34)*
> *But he was wounded for our transgressions, he was bruised for our iniquities; the chastisement of our peace was upon him and with his stripes we are healed. (Isaiah 53:5)*

187

Throughout the Bible, we find countless portions of scripture showing our God is a faithful God who never fails to keep His word. He has already paid for your healing on the Cross of Calvary! Do not allow the Devil to lie to you. Regardless of how your body may feel, healing for your physical body is a done deal.

The Bible tells us that after we follow the key steps laid down by the Spirit of God then and only then will the promise be manifested "and the Lord shall raise him up." That is to say, if we do our part then God will assuredly perform His part. Why not give the word of God a chance in your situation? It will blow your mind what God can do for you!

HE WILL WASH AWAY YOUR SINS

Seventh, as a result of our obedience and completion of the key steps for believer's physical healing and total restoration, the Lord did not promise to only heal our physical body, He also promised that if we "have committed sins, they shall be forgiven him." (James 5:15) Our heavenly Father's perfect will and good pleasure is for us to be made completely whole. The Lord Jesus Christ is not interested in a partly-delivered person. He is interested in the wholeness of a complete person.

The Bible tells us, "When Jesus saw their faith, he said unto sick of the palsy, Son, thy sins be forgiven thee" (Mark 2:5). From this portion of the scripture we see that the Lord is not only interested in physical healing, He also wants to redeem our soul. The Lord healed this man with palsy and forgave his sins. He is waiting to do the same for you today.

These are the seven key steps for a believer's physical healing and total restoration. It is my earnest prayer they will be a great blessing to you.

THREE REQUIREMENTS TO MAINTAIN YOUR HEALING

One thing I have seen in the Church is that many children of God receive physical healing after they were prayed for but lose it after a short period of time. Why does this happen? It is because they failed to maintain the healing they received. In order for us to retain physical healing, there are three things that we must do.

First, we must be thoroughly grounded and immersed in the word of God. This means you must know what the "will" of God is concerning "Divine Health" for you and your household. The Bible tells us, "And ye shall know the truth and the truth shall make you free." (John 8:32) It is the truth you know, in the word of God, that makes you free. You must fill and occupy your heart with the powerful words of God in order to maintain and keep your physical healing. The word of God gives us this precious advice,

> *My son attend to my words; incline thine ear unto my sayings. Let them not depart from thine eyes; keep them in the midst of thine heart. For they are life to those that find them, and health to all their flesh. Keep thy heart with all diligence; for out of it are the issues of life. (Proverbs 4:20-23(*
> *And there was delivered into Him the book of the prophet Esaias. And when He had opened the book, He found the place where it was written (Luke 4:17)*

Therefore, in order for us to maintain physical healing and complete restoration, we must hide the word of God, the healing scriptures [promises of God] inside our hearts where they will protect and maintain the healing we received from God.

We note that the book of the Prophet Isaiah was given to the Lord Jesus Christ when He entered the temple. When He opened the book He found what was written concerning Himself many years before He was born. The point here is that He had to open the book to discover. In like manner, we must open the Bible so we can find the promises of God that have been written for us. God wants us to live in divine health but sometimes we do not know it. The Devil robs us of what belongs to us because we do not know what belongs to us. We cannot have what we do not believe is rightfully ours. We must search the scripture to discover our heritage!

Second, we must have faith and full confidence in the word of God and believe that it has the power to do great work for us. This means that we must put all our trust in the word of God.

Third, in order to obtain, maintain, and retain physical healing, we must continuously "act upon" the word of God. The Bible tells us "Faith without works is dead." (James 2:26) This is the vital key thing we must do to help us "obtain, maintain, and retain" the physical healing we receive through the power of prayer. Many children of God "obtain" their physical healing when they are prayed for but ironically loose it thereafter because they are not fully furnished with the word of God to help them sustain healing.

HOW TO POSSESS AND CONFESS YOUR HEALING INTO REALITY

Based on my daily walk and relationship with the Lord and coupled with my experiences, I have observed that there are two major ways that our God administers physical healing to His children. It is either an "Instant healing manifestation" or a "gradual healing manifestation." Either way, it is the Lord's good "will" to manifest a healing touch on His children. The word of God tells us,

> And this is the confidence that we have in Him, that, if we ask any thing according to His will, He heareth us. And if we know that He hear us, whatsoever we ask, we know that we have the partitions that we desired of Him. (1 John 5:14-15)

This is one of the greatest promises for the children of God in the entire Bible. It guarantees believers that if they shall ask any thing according to the "will" of God it will be given to them. Based upon this scripture, it is the responsibility of the believers to search the scripture for the "will" of God in any situation they face. When we find out what the "will" of God is, we can boldly and confidently approach the throne room of God, in prayer, knowing that "we have the petitions that we desired from Him." The scripture tells us:

> Therefore I say unto you, what things soever ye desire, when ye pray, believe that ye have it and ye shall receive it. (Mark 11:24)

Whatever we have need of, when we asked for it in prayer according to the "will" of God, we must believe has been given to us the very moment we asked for it. This includes physical healing for our body. After we pray for the healing of our physical body, we maintain, protect, and keep the healing we receive by faith and by feeding our spirit with the word of God, mediating and confessing. To help us do exactly that, let's study some of the healing scriptures in the Bible.

THE HEALING SCRIPTURES

The Bible teaches that we can receive any thing from God by faith in His spoken word. That is, we must know the word of God, believe on the word of God and act on the word of God. In the same manner, we must obtain, maintain, and retain our physical healing by resting on the word of God. The Bible tells us that:

> *Heaven and earth shall pass away but my words shall not pass away.*
> (Matthew 34:35)

Not only must we know what God has to say concerning our physical healing but to maintain and keep our healing we must couple our knowledge of the word of God with acting on the word and confessing the word which we believe.

The following healing scriptures can help you stand on the word of the living God. They will boost your faith and help you believe God for the manifestation of healing. Let's prayerfully believe and feed on these and other portions of healing scripture and watch God perform His word upon us.

> *How God anointed Jesus of Nazareth with the Holy Ghost and with power: who went about doing good, and healing all that were oppressed of the Devil; for God was with him.*
> *(Acts 10:38)*

Behold, I am the Lord, the God of all flesh: is there any thing too hard for me? (Jeremiah 32:27)

Is any sick among you? Let him call for the elders of the church; and let them pray over him, anointing him with oil in the name of the Lord. And the prayer of faith shall save the sick, and the Lord shall raise him up; and if he has committed sins, they shall be forgiven him. (James 5:14-15)

My son, attend to my words; incline thine ear unto my sayings. Let them not depart from thine eyes; keep them in the midst of thine heart. For they are life unto those that find them, and health to all their flesh. Keep thy heart with all diligence, for out of it are the issues of life. (Proverbs 4:20-23)

He sent his word, and healed them, and delivered them from their destructions. (Psalms 107:20)

Who his own self bore our sins in his own body on the tree, that we, being dead to sins, should live unto righteousness: by whose stripes ye were healed. (1 Peter 2:24)

Surely he hath borne our griefs, and carried our sorrow: yet we did esteem him stricken, smitten of God, and afflicted. But he was wounded for our transgressions, he was bruised for our iniquities: the chastisement of our peace was upon him; and with his stripes we are healed. (Isaiah 53:4-5)

That it might be fulfilled which was spoken by Esais the prophet, saying,

Himself took our infirmities, and bare our sicknesses. (Matthew 8:17)

Bless the Lord, O my soul: and all that is within me bless his holy name. Bless the Lord, O my soul, and forget not all his benefits. Who forgiveth all thine iniquities; and who healeth all thine diseases. (Psalms 103:1-3)

And said, if thou wilt diligently hearken to the voice of the Lord thy God, and wilt do that which is right in his sight, and wilt give ear to his commandments, and keep all his status, I will put none of these diseases upon thee, which I have brought upon the Egyptians: for I am the Lord that healeth thee.
(Exodus 15:26)

Have mercy upon me, O Lord; for I am weak: O Lord, heal me; for my bones are vexed. (Psalms 6:2)

This book of the law shall not depart out of thy mouth; but thou shall meditate therein day and night, that thou mayest observe to do according to all that is written therein: for then thou shall make thy way prosperous, and then thou shall have good success. (Joshua 1:8)

Child of God, I am confident that if you diligently feed your spirit with the word of the Lord, and meditate on it fervently, it has the power to turn your situation around. Why not give it a chance?

WHY NOT GIVE JESUS CHRIST A CHANCE?

The Bible emphatically tells us that the key to

victorious living is obedience to the spoken words of God. In fact, the only way we can experience the wonder working power of the living God in our lives is to obey and act upon the words of God. The Lord tells us:

> *"If ye be willing and obedient, ye shall eat the good of the land. But if ye refuse and rebel ye shall be devoured with the sword: for the mouth of the Lord hath spoken it. (Isaiah 1:19-20)*
> *Come unto me all ye that labor and are of heavy laden and I will give you rest. (Matthew 11:28)*

This is an open invitation to whomsoever comes. It is the Lord's good pleasure to give His children peace and rest in every aspect of their lives. Whatever challenges of life we go through, we can count on the Lord to be there with us.

You may be carrying a heavy load of sin, sickness, fear, poverty, future uncertainty, hopelessness, depression, anxiety, failure, sexual addiction, drug addiction and rejection. I have good news for you. The Lord wants to take your heavy load and give you peace of mind. All you have to do is honor and accept the Lord's invitation. "Come unto Him" with your heavy load and "He will give you rest." Millions have honored this open invitation and the Lord had not disappointed them and He will not disappoint you. Why not give the Lord a chance today?.

My dear friend, I want you to know that what the Lord did for other people, He can do for you. Let us take a closer look at the two individuals who came to the Lord Jesus Christ for physical healing. It is my prayer that this miraculous healing event will stir your faith to believe God for the miracle you desperately need. The scripture tells us of a woman who had a very terrible physical condition.

> *And a certain woman, which had an issue of blood twelve years. And had suffered many things of many physicians, and had spent all that she had, and was not bettered, but rather grew worse. When she had heard of Jesus, came in the press behind, and touched his garment. For she said, if I may touch but his clothes, I shall be whole. And straightway the fountain of he blood was dried up; and she felt in her body that she was healed of her plague. (Mark 5:25-29)*

Child of God, whatever physical illness the Devil may have inflicted on your body and whatever bad news your doctor may have given to you, I have good news! Your doctor does not have the last word, God does!

The Bible tells us this woman suffered terribly with a disease in her blood cells for twelve years. She had endured many attempts at cures by many physicians but her condition grew worse instead of better. She spent every thing she had. According to the Bible, this woman was in very bad shape. She had done every thing she knew but to no avail. She had every reason to give up hope, stay in bed and wait for death. But she refused to give up. She was a fighter!

When she heard Jesus was in town, she decided that if she could but touch the garment of Jesus Christ she would be made whole and when she did, she was made completely whole. There are some valuable lessons to obtain from the physical healing of this woman that we can apply to any situation we face today.

First, this woman received her miracle healing because she "came" to the one who is able to do all things well. Second, she received her miracle healing because she came to Jesus Christ with "expectation." Child of God, I believe wholeheartedly that what the Lord did for this woman, because she came to Him with faith and expectation, He will do for anyone who comes to Him.

Therefore, whatever you may be going through today, all you need to do is come to the Lord and He will give you rest. This woman came to the Lord because she heard of how the Lord had cleansed the lepers, turned water into wine, and used five loaves of bread and two little fish to feed five thousand men (not counting women and children.) The scripture tells us "So then faith cometh by hearing by the word of God" (Romans 10:17). My dear friend, I trust that the revelation and information you have received has been a great blessing to you.

Chapter 13

DOWN DOESN'T MEAN OUT

The steps of a good man are ordered by the Lord: and he delighteth in his way. Though he fall, he shall not be utterly cast down: for the Lord upoldeth him with his hand. (Psalm 37:23-24)

The scripture and our everyday experience prove to us that life is a long journey and our days are spent in constant battles. Nowhere in the pages of the Bible, does the Lord promise His children a battle-free life. However, He assuredly guarantees us a defeat-free life. The Bible tells us *"But thanks be to God, who gives us the victory through Jesus Christ."* (1 Corinthians 15:57) When the Bible says that God has already given us victory, through Jesus Christ, it is incorrect to assume that our lives will be battle-free. In fact many people, especially new believers in Christ, wrongfully assume that as soon as they become Christians they will begin to live a battle-free life. That is really not the case! I wish it were the case!

In fact, the beginning of our walk and relationship with God, through the Lord Jesus Christ, signals the beginning of our battle with the flesh, sin, lust, the Devil and his powerless agents. Child of God, let there be no mistake regarding the fact that as we journey in this life we are going to battle the issues of life.

Job, in one of his writings, emphatically stated for our exhortation that, *"Man that is born of a woman is of few days, and full of trouble"(Job 14:1).* In addition, King David pointed out that *"Many are the affliction of the righteous but the Lord delivereth him from them all. He keepeth his bones, not one of them is broken" (Psalm 34:19-20).* Therefore as children of God, we should expect challenges in life just like others not under the covenant blood of the Lord Jesus Christ. We must never forget that we are fighting for victory but not fighting to win. We are already winners through the blood of the Lord!

In our conflicts we may be knocked down but not destroyed, as the Apostle Paul clearly wrote to the Corinthian Christians. We must never be alarmed or feel that we are alone because *"greater is he that is in you than he that is in the world."* (1John 4:4) There are times, in each one of our lives, that issues overwhelm us and weigh us down. That is because troubles and problems are part of the human race!

There is no question that every child of God will be tested. Oh, yes, our faith will now and then go through fire! In such difficult times there is a tendency and temptation to get discouraged, cast down, and give up hope. I have good news for you! When the issues of life overwhelm you "encourage yourself" in the Lord your God.

Remind yourself what God has already done for you. Remember how He healed, protected, delivered you from destruction, rescued you, fought your battles, and sustained you. As you look back at all the Lord has done for you; faith, joy and the peace of

God will overwhelm you.

Also, as you begin to *"put off the spirit of heaviness and put on the garment of praise"* (Isaiah 61:3) your soul will be revived and refreshed. There is no doubt about it! When we are overwhelmed and discouraged and even cast down with the issues and battles of life, when we begin to praise God for all He has done we come alive again. Praise to God will dispel discouragement!

Therefore, being down does not mean that you are out! You can praise your way out of discouragement and heaviness. Give it a chance! As we shall see later, when we praise God for what He has done for us, especially in times when we are discouraged and downcast, the Devil and his forces cannot withstand the spirit of praise. When we praise God He comes upon us to inhabit our praise, *"But thou art holy, O thou that inhabitest the praises of Israel"* (Psalm 22:3). This means that God will come and "sit" with us because the power of our praises to Him makes the evil spirits depart. Praise draws the presence of God unto those who praise Him, and expels the spirit of heaviness that brings discouragement.

Let us look closely at another time that great King David was down, discouraged, and almost out and see how he overcame. The Bible tells us:

> *I will say unto God my rock, why hast thou forgotten me? Why go I mourning because of the oppression of my enemy? As with a sword in my bones, my enemies reproach me; while they say daily unto me, where is thy God? Why art thou cast down, O my soul? and why art thou disquieted within me? Hope thou in God: for I shall yet praise Him, who is the health of my*

countenance, and my God.
(Psalm 42:9-11)

Child of God, we can see how King David overcame his discouragement. We see that King David gathered himself together and encouraged himself in the Lord his God. In fact, after gathering himself together, he began to rebuke his soul for being down and disquieted within him. He stirred himself and encouraged himself to praise and hope in God.

This is the key for our total victory over the Devil and his forces when they oppress us with the spirit of heaviness and try to steal our trust and hope in God. We must do what the Apostle Paul and great King David did when they were down, discouraged, and almost out. They strengthened, encouraged, and put their hopes back on the Lord.

As you read this book, you may be faced with what seem to be insurmountable issues of life. Why not remind yourself of all the Lord's goodness towards you? Why not count your blessings and name them one after the other? As you do, faith and strength will rise within you! What God did for great King David and the Apostle Paul He will do for you if you do what they did when they were down.

The Bible also tells us about another prophet of God named Elijah who suffered with discouragement, was cast down, but not out.

> *And Ahab told Jezebel all that Elijah*
> *had done, and withal how he had slain*
> *all the prophet with the sword. Then*
> *Jezebel sent a messenger unto Elijah,*
> *saying, so let the gods do to me, and*
> *more also, if I make not thy life as the*
> *life of one of them by tomorrow about*

this time. And when he saw that, he arose, and went for his life, and came to Beersheba, which belongeth to Judah, and left his servant there. But he himself went a day's journey into the wilderness, and came and sat under a juniper tree: and he requested for himself that he might die; and said, it is enough; now, O LORD, take away my life; for I am not better than my fathers. And as he lay and slept under a juniper tree, behold, then an angel touched him, and said unto him, arise and eat. And he looked, and, behold, there was a cake baking on the coal, and cruse of water at his head. And he did eat and drink, and laid him down again. And the angel of the LORD came again the second time, and touched him, and said, arise and eat; because the journey is too great for thee.   (1 Kings 19:1-7)

As we see, from the above portions of scripture, some times the journey of life takes a U-turn or is like a curve ball thrown into the life of God's children. In fact, as the sun shines upon both the just and unjust, and as the rain falls on the fields of both the righteous and the unrighteous, even so are the troubles and issues of life. They come upon all of us. In the case of Elijah, a great prophet of the living God, the Bible tells us he had an encounter with the ungodly prophets of Baal and slaughtered them. When the news got to the ears of Jezebel, the wife of King Ahab of Israel, she went after the life of Elijah.

When Elijah heard that Jezebel was looking for him he ran for his life, terribly discouraged and down. He even requested that God would take his life. It was very obvious that Elijah was discouraged and down but he was not in danger because God had him covered.

God did not forget or forsake him. He was with Elijah in his weakest moment to help and restore him. Child of God, we are serving a living and loving God who would never leave us nor forsake us regardless of our state of being. We must never take our eyes away from the living God.

It should not surprise us to know that life is not perfect. There are going to be several detours along the way. Those detours may bring disappointment, frustration, hopelessness, discouragement, and lost of trust in God. Whatever issues may have brought you hopelessly down and discouraged, all you need to find your way out is to: (1) Encourage yourself in the Lord (remind yourself of what the Lord has done for you. This will cause faith to come alive within you. (2) Put off the spirit of heaviness by putting on the garment of praise (3) Sing praises unto God and draw upon His presence because God's presence drives out the Devil and his forces

PRAISE DRIVES THE DEVIL CRAZY AND BRINGS DELIVERANCE

We find volumes of biblical evidence on how God used the power of praise to bring tremendous victories to His children. Let us look at a few examples to encourage faith to believe God for the impossibilities in our own lives. Child of God, remember that God is no respecter of persons. What He did for others He will do for you.

When you are down and hopelessly discouraged, what you need to do first is what brings "hope" back into your being.

PRAISE PRODUCES JOY AND STRENGTH

For the joy of the Lord is our strength. (Nehemiah 8:10)

A merry heart maketh a cheerful countenance: but by sorrow of the heart the spirit is broken. (Proverbs 15:13)

Rejoice in the Lord, O ye righteous: for praise is comely for the upright. Praise the Lord harp: sing unto Him with the psaltery and with instrument of ten strings.. Sing unto Him a new song: play skillfully with a loud noise.
(Psalm 33:1-4)

Praise ye the Lord. praise, O ye servants of the Lord, praise the name of the Lord. Blessed be the name of the Lord from this time forth and for evermore. From the rising of the sun unto the going down of the same the Lord's name is to be praise.
(Psalm 113:1-3)

I will bless the Lord at all times: His praise shall continually be in my mouth. My soul shall make her boast in the Lord: the humble shall hear thereof, and be glad. O magnify the Lord with me, and let us exalt His name together.
(Psalm 34:1-3)

A merry heart doth good like a medicine: but a broken spirit drieth the bones. (Proverbs 17:22)

Make a joyful noise unto the Lord, all ye lands. Serve the Lord with gladness: come before His presence with singing. Enter into His gates with thanksgiving, and into His court with praise: be

thankful unto Him, and bless His name.
(Psalm 100:1-3 &4)

When the Devil battles with you to snatch away your "hope", praise the name of the living God. This will drive him and his forces crazy and expel him from you. Oh, yes, you can praise your way out of anything the Devil brings against you! There are volumes of facts, throughout the Bible, confirming that praise expels and destroys the Devil and his ugly devices. For example, the Bible tell us:

> *But the spirit of the Lord departed from Saul, and an evil spirit from the Lord troubled him. And Saul's servants said unto him, behold now, an evil spirit from God troubleth thee. It came to pass, when the evil spirit from God was upon Saul, that David took a harp, and played with his hand: so Saul was refreshed, and was well, and the evil spirit departed from him.*
> *(1 Samuel 16:14-16 &23)*
> *And at midnight Paul and Silas prayed, and sang praises unto God: and the prisoners heard them. And suddenly there was a great earthquake, so that the foundations of the prison were shaken: and immediately all the doors were opened, and everyone's bonds were loosed.*
> *(Acts 16:25-26)*

Child of God, there is no doubt what the power of praise can do, especially in difficult times. We see in the above portions of the scripture how the power of praise brought total deliverance for King Saul. After

Saul sinned against God and God rejected him from continuing as ruler of His people Israel, the Bible tells us God allowed an evil spirit to enter him. When young David was brought in with his harp to sing praises unto the Lord, the evil spirit that was in King Saul departed from him. This is because the Devil cannot stand in the presence of the living God.

Whenever you are down and almost out, all you need to do is gather yourself, begin reminding yourself of all the goodness God has brought into your life in the past and then sing praises unto His holy name. I assure you, by the authority of the God's word, that when you do this the presence of God will invade your life and expel the Devil and his devices. God did it for King Saul and He will do it for you.

The Bible also tells us when the Apostle Paul and his companion, Silas, were arrested for preaching the gospel of the Lord Jesus Christ they were bound with chains and put into the inner prison. In human nature they would have been discouraged but the Bible tells us at midnight they rose up, prayed and sang praises unto the Lord. Because praise invites the presence of God, the presence of God came and shook the prison from its foundation. The bonds and chains with which they were secured broke off them. They were miraculously delivered because they prayed and sang praises unto God who inhabits the praises of His children.

It is important to note that when the Apostles Paul and Silas sang, the Bible tells us the other prisoners and jailers heard them. Some times, it is important for us to make our affirmation known to people, regardless of the situation in which we find ourselves. There is power in praise. So when the Devil gets you cornered, remember that praising God will restore your hope, trust and also bring the deliverance that you earnestly need. You may be down right now, but you are not out because God's got you covered.

PRAISE BRINGS DESTRUCTION UPON YOUR ENEMIES

Praise not only brings restoration, joy, hope, strength and deliverance from the hands of your enemies it also brings great destruction upon their heads. Regardless of what your enemies throw at you, you can praise your way out of all the pits, weapons, traps and snares they have set up against your life. Let's look at an example of the power of Praise at work in a time of trouble for the children of God. The Bible tells us:

> *It came to pass after this also, that the children of Moab, and the children of Ammon, and with them beside the Ammonites, came against Jehoshaphat to battle. Then there came some that told Jehoshaphat, saying, There cometh a great multitude against thee from beyond the sea on this side Syria: and, behold, they be in Hazazontamar, which is Engedi. And Jehoshaphat feared, and set himself to seek the Lord, and proclaimed a fast throughout all Judah. And Judah gathered themselves together, to ask help of the Lord: even out of all the cities of Judah they came to seek the Lord. And Jehoshaphat stood in the congregation of Judah and Jerusalem, in the house of the Lord, before the new court, And said, O Lord God of our fathers, art not thou God in heaven? And rulest not*

thou over all the kingdoms of the heathen? And in thine hand is there not power and might, so that none is able to withstand thee? Art not thou our God, who didst drive out the inhabitants of this land before they people Israel, and gavest it to the seed of Abraham they friend forever? And they dwelt therein, and have built thee a sanctuary therein, and have built thee a sanctuary therein for thy name, saying, If, when evil cometh upon us, as the sword, judgment, or pestilence, or famine, we stand before this house, and in thy presence, (for thy name is in the house,) and cry unto thee in our affliction, then thou wilt hear and help. And now, behold, the children of Ammon and Moab and mount Seir, whom thou wouldest not let Israel invade, when they came out of the land of Egypt, but they turned from them, and they destroyed them not; Behold, I say, how they reward us, to come to cast us out of thy possession, which thou hast given us to inherit. O our God, wilt thou not judge them? For we have no might against this great company that cometh against us; neither know we what to do: but our eyes are upon thee. And all Judah stood before the Lord, with their little ones, their wives, and their children. Then upon Jahaziel the son of Zechariah, the son of Benaiah, the son of Jeiel, the son of Mattaniah, a levite of the sons of Asaph, came the spirit of the Lord in the midst of the congregation; And he said, Hearken ye, all Judah, and ye inhabitants of Jerusalem, and thou king Jehoshaphat, Thus saith the Lord unto you, Be not afraid nor dismayed by reason of this great multitude; for the battle is not yours, but God's. Tomorrow go ye down against them: behold, they come up by the cliff of Zip; and ye shall find them at the end of the brook, before the wilderness of Ferule. Ye shall not need to fight in this battle: set yourselves, stand ye still, and see the salvation of the Lord with you, O Judah and Jerusalem: fear not, nor be dismayed; tomorrow go out against them: for the Lord will be with you. And Jehoshaphat bowed his head with his face to the ground: and all Judah and the inhabitants of Jerusalem fell before the Lord, worshipping the Lord. And the Levites, of the children of the Kohathites, and of the children of the Korhites, stood up to praise the Lord God of Israel with a loud voice on high. And they rose early in the morning, and went forth into the wilderness of Tekoa: and as they went forth, Jehoshaphat stood and said, Hear me, O Judah, and ye inhabitants of Jerusalem; Believe in the Lord your God, so shall ye be established; believe his prophets, so shall ye prosper. And when he had consulted with the people, he appointed singers unto the Lord, and that should praise the beauty of holiness, and they went out before the army, and to say, Praise the Lord; for his mercy endureth forever. And when they began to sing and to praise, the Lord set ambushes against the children of Ammon, Moab, and mount Seir, which come against Judah; and they were smitten. For the children of Ammon and Moab stood up against the inhabitants of mount Seir, utterly to slay and destroy them: and when they had made an end of the inhabitants of Seir, every one helped to destroy another. And when Judah came toward the watchtower in the wilderness, they looked unto the multitude, and, behold, they were dead bodies fallen to the earth, and none escaped. And when Jehoshaphat and his people came to take away the spoil of them, they found among them in abundance both riches with the dead bodies, and precious jewels, which they stripped off for themselves, more than they could carry away: and they were three days in gathering of the spoil, it was so much. And on the fourth day they assembled themselves in the valley of Berachah; for there they blessed the Lord: therefore the name of the same place was called, the valley of Berachah, unto this day. Then they returned, every man of Judah and Jerusalem, and Jehoshaphat in the forefront of them, to go again to Jerusalem with joy; for the Lord had made them to rejoice over their enemies. And they came to Jerusalem with psalteries and harps and trumpets unto the house of Lord. And the fear of God was on all the kingdoms of those countries, when they had heard that the Lord fought against the enemies of Israel. So the realm of Jehoshaphat was quiet: for his God gave him rest round about. (2 Chronicles 20:1-30)

There are three valuable lessons to learn from this encounter between King Jehoshaphat and the three nations that came against him.

- First, King Jehoshaphat recognized that only God could help them out of their troubles.
- Second, King Jehoshaphat and the people in his kingdom purposed in their hearts to seek the face of God.
- Third, God gave them instructions for victory. God Almighty gave them victory over their enemies because they called upon Him for help!

Regardless of the circumstances you face today, the same God who delivered King Jehoshaphat and his people is still on the throne to deliver you from the hands of your enemies. Call upon Him, seek His face and He will give you instruction for the victory you desperately need.

Chapter 14

OBEDIENCE IS YOUR KEY TO VICTORY

So Naaman came with his horses and with his chariot, and stood at the door of the house of Elisha. And Elisha sent a messenger unto him, saying, Go and wash in Jordan seven times, and thy flesh shall come again to thee, and thou shalt be clean. (2 Kings 5:9-10)
His mother saith unto the servants, whatsoever he saith unto you, do it. (John 2:5)
Then Peter and the other apostles answered and said, we ought to obey God rather than man. (Acts 5:29)

In this chapter, we take a closer look at the lives of ordinary people in the Bible. We will see how God miraculously turned insurmountable circumstances around because of their obedience to the voice and instruction of God's words. I believe your faith will be challenged, provoked, and strengthened to trust and believe God for your impossibilities and the breakthrough you desperately need today. God wants to stretch and move you to the next level but He cannot do it without your cooperation and obedience to His instructions.

Therefore your key to breakthrough is obedience to the commands and instructions of God. Since our *"God is no respecter of persons"* (Acts 10;34) He will do for you what he Has done for others if you do what others did that allowed God to bless them. Let us, with an attitude of expectation, look closely and carefully into the lives of these individuals to see how God turned circumstances and challenges around because they dared to obey the word of God.

It is biblically obvious that the blessing of God come upon our lives as a result of faith and obedience to the words of God. Child of God, remember that our circumstances do not move God at all, but our faith and obedience in His word do. Regardless of what you may be going through today, all you need to receive your breakthrough is faith and obedience in the words of the living God.

If we refuse to believe that God, through the blood of the Lord Jesus Christ, has already paid for our physical healing we can never be healed of any illness that the Devil may put upon our lives. It will not matter how much we are prayed for.

Also, if you refuse to believe that salvation of souls is only by faith in the shed blood of the Lord Jesus Christ and not by good works done, the promises of God cannot manifest in your life. Therefore, we must be willing to obey and be submissive to the words of God in order to see the manifestation of God's power in our lives.

The Bible records, for our exhortation and faith building, an encounter between our Lord Jesus Christ, his mother Mary and servants of the bridegroom at Cana of Galilee.

And third day there was a marriage in Cana of Galilee; and the mother of Jesus was there. And both Jesus was called (invited), and His disciples, to the marriage. And when they wanted wine, the mother of Jesus saith unto Him, they have no wine. Jesus saith unto her, Woman, what have I to do with thee, mine hour is not yet come. His mother saith unto the servants, whatsoever He saith unto thee, do it. And there were sitting there six water pots of stone, after the manner of the purifying of the Jews, containing two or three firkins apiece. Jesus saith unto them, fill the pots with water. And they filled them up to the brim. And He saith unto them, draw out now, and bear unto the governor of the feast. And they bore it. When the ruler of the feast had tasted the water that was made wine, (he knew not whence it came but the servants which drew the water knew) the governor of the feast called the bridegroom. And saith unto him, every one at the beginning doth set forth good wine: and when men had well drunk, then that which is worse: but thou hast kept the good wine until now. This beginning of miracle did Jesus in Cana of Galilee, and manifested forth His glory: and His disciples believed on Him. (John 2:1-11)

Child of God, as we see, this wonderful and spectacular miracle came into reality as a result of obedience. The servants of the bridegroom followed the instructions of Jesus. There are crucial and valuable lessons to learn from this miracle encounter. They will help build our faith to believe God for whatever breakthrough we desire of the Lord.

First, Mary, the mother of Jesus knew whom to turn to in a time of need. A quick question before we proceed. Who do you turn to when you are faced with the troubles and issues of life? Ironically, many of us fail to go to the "Master of all Situations" when we run into trouble. Most often, some of us exhaust every other means we have before turning to the Lord Jesus Christ. In other words, we run to God after other means have failed! It ought not to be so! Just as Mary did when a crisis arose, we as the children of God should always turn to the Lord Jesus Christ first, not as a last resort.

Secondly, Mary instructed the servants of the bridegroom *"Whatsoever He saith unto you, do it."* She emphatically urged the bridegroom's servants to obey the words of His mouth. This is very significant because she was aware that the words He would speak *" they are spirit and they are life." (John 6:63)* She also wanted them to be prepared to obey because she understood the miracle breakthrough they needed depended wholly on their obedience to the words of His mouth. In fact, Mary believed that there was power in the words of the living God and that they had the ability to perform what they were sent to do.

Child of God, in the same manner, we must believe and have unwavering and unshakeable confidence in the word of God that He will do what He has promised to do for us. Just as Mary forewarned the servants of the bridegroom to be prepared for the miracle they needed, even so I am led by the Spirit of God to prepare you, the reader of this book, to build up your faith so you can believe

God for your breakthrough.

Thirdly, the Lord Jesus Christ instructed the servants to do what seemed to make no common sense. Child of God, remember they needed wine to entertain the guests of honor at the wedding. Our Lord commanded them to fill six empty water pots with ordinary water. They simply obeyed, without any arguments, questions, or reservations. Although there was little correlation between what they needed (wine to entertain their guests of honor) and what the Lord asked them to do, they simply obeyed the commands and did it anyway. When they did, the miracle took place. Praise God! Did not the scripture say, *"Obedience is better than sacrifice?"* (1Samuel 15:22)

There are many biblical examples showing sometimes the Lord directs us to do things that are not ordinary nor make any common sense. If we dare to obey His instructions, we will see power and glory manifested in our lives! The servants obeyed the instructions of the Lord to fill the pots with ordinary water and gave it to the ruler of the feast without any hesitation or reservation. Thank God they did because the Bible tells us when they obeyed a miracle was manifested to the glory of God and to the amazement of all who attended the wedding ceremony.

I want you to note carefully that this miracle came to pass because supernatural God and natural men worked together in total agreement. The Lord did not do it alone! I hope this statement does not shock you! The Bible says, *"Can two walk together except they be agreed?" (Amos 3:3).* There is no question that the only scriptural way we can continuously experience the manifestation of power and glory in our lives is to walk in total obedience and agreement with God. The natural men (servants of the

217

bridegroom) did what they were capable of doing, that is to "fill the empty water pots with water" and the supernatural Lord turned the water into sweet wine to meet their needs.

This principle is very important! If we obediently do what we are capable of doing, as instructed by the Lord, then the Lord will do for us what we are not capable of doing. When natural mankind and supernatural God come together, in total agreement, mind-blowing miracles will take place.

Let us ponder this crucial point for a moment. What if the servants of this bridegroom, who had never heard about the Lord Jesus Christ, had failed to obey His instructions? Could this miracle have been possible? The answer is a resounding no!

However, if the Lord miraculously meets the needs of these servants, who had no personal relationships with Him whatsoever, how much more will He meet the needs of those of us washed with His precious Blood and having a personal relationship with Him? I tell you the truth He is more eager to bless us than we are willing to believe. Therefore, regardless of what your needs or circumstances may be, you can have the breakthrough you desperately need from God. You must be prepared to obey His instructions and be submissive to the leading and guidance of the Spirit of God. If you seek His face and call for help, in His name, God will give you instructions for your breakthrough!

HE OBEYED AND WAS HEALED

Let us look at another person, in the Bible, whose insurmountable situation was miraculously turned around because of simple obedience to the word of God. The Bible tells us:

So Naaman came with his horses and with his chariot, and stood at the door of the house of Elisha. And Elisha sent a messenger unto him, saying, go and wash in Jordan seven times, and thy flesh shall come again to thee, and thou shall be clean. But Naaman was wroth, and said, behold, I thought, he will surely come out to me, and stand, and call on the name of the Lord his God, and strike his hand over the place, and recover the leper. Are not Abana and Pharpar, rivers of Damascus, better than all the waters of Israel? May I not wash in them, and be clean? So he turned and went away in a rage. And his servants came near, and spake unto him, and said, my father, if the people had bid thee do some great thing, wouldest thou not have done it? How much rather then, when he saith to thee, wash, and be clean? Then went he down, and dipped himself seven times in the Jordan, according to the saying of the man of God: And his flesh came again like unto the flesh of a little child, and he was clean.
(2 Kings 5:9-14)

We saw earlier how the Jesus used the simple faith and obedience of the bridegroom's servants to turn six pots of water into wine. The story affirms that all we need to live a victorious life is obedience to the living God. From the portion of scripture above, we find another person, Naaman.

The Bible tells us that Naaman was a captain in

the army of Syria. From all that we know about him, he was second in command, next to the king of Syria. He was a man of high repute and well recognized and respected throughout the land of Syria. He also carried a heavy load in life. He was a leper.

In ancient times it was customary practice that any person with leprosy must automatically become an outcast. This meant that the person would no longer be counted as part of the society and was excluded from the general population. They were sent to a secluded place designated for such people as long as he or she lived.

This was not the fate of Naaman because he was most loved by the king of Syria. Because of his reputation and important military position in the government of Syria, he was given preferential treatment and was not cast away nor secluded.

In one of the wars with Israel the Syrian army, led by Naaman, defeated the army of Israel and took many captives. The Bible tells us that God allowed the armies of Israel to be defeated because of their sins and rebellion against God and because of their refusal to repent of their wicked ways. One of those taken captive was a young girl Naaman chose to be a maid for his wife. While the little captive girl was playing with her fellow maids she told them there was a Prophet of God, in the land of Israel, who could cure Naaman of his leprosy. Immediately, the news was brought to the attention of Naaman and then to the king of Syria.

When the king of Syria heard of this possibility he sent a letter to the king of Israel, with Naaman, in which he requested him to help Naaman recover from leprosy. The Bible records that when Naaman, with his entourage, came to the king of Israel and delivered the letter, the King Israel tore his clothes in rage. According to the Bible,

It came to pass, when the King of Israel had read the letter that he rent his clothes, and said, "Am I God, to kill and make alive, that this man doth send unto me to recover a man of his leprosy? Wherefore consider I pray you, and see how he seeketh a quarrel against me." And it was so when Elisha the man God had heard that the King of Israel had rent his clothes, that he sent to the King, saying, "Wherefore hast thou rent thy clothes? Let him come now to me, and he shall know that there is prophet in Israel." (2 Kings 5:7-8)

So, the king of Israel sent Naaman to meet Elisha. When he arrived at the door, Elisha sent his messenger to meet him. He told Naaman to go to the Jordan River and dip himself seven times and then his leprosy would disappear. Naaman was outraged and terribly disappointed because the man of God did not come out of his house to meet with him, lay his hand upon him and call upon God to heal him. He was greatly displeased and left the house of Elisha, very angry. One of his servants pleaded with him and convinced him to obey the instructions of the man of God and act on them. The Bible tells us that he then reluctantly obeyed and followed the instructions. When he did, his leprosy left his body by the power of the living God. He received new flesh like the flesh of a child. Praise God! It was a wonderful miracle realized as a result of obedience to the words of God.

Naaman almost missed his miracle healing because of disobedience. We also see that Naaman was greatly disappointed because his expectation of how he would be healed. The man of God will "surely come out and lay his hand on me and call on his God to heal me" he thought.

Earlier I pointed out that when we come to the Lord with our life needs, the Lord will sometimes give us instructions that may not make any sense. If we are willing and obedient, we will receive the breakthrough from the Lord. Let us face it, the instructions Elisha, the man of God, gave to Naaman did not make any common sense. After all, Naaman and his entourage traveled hundreds of miles from the land of Syria to the land of Israel. How did the man of God dare instruct Naaman to go to the dirty river of Jordan to dip himself seven times? "Are there not better rivers in Syria than the river Jordan," he angrily asked? What Naaman did not understood was that God is the King of all kings and that no one tells Him what to do and how He should do it. He is God and we are not!

Child of God, it is very important that we never try to put God in a box. We must always rest in His infinite wisdom and power to manifest themselves on our behalf. Naaman went to the Jordan, halfheartedly, and dipped himself seven times as the man of God had instructed him to do. His leprosy left his body and new flesh was miraculously given to him. The key to any victory is obedience to the voice of God. Regardless of circumstances and challenges that come our way, as we journey in life, all we need to achieve our breakthrough is obedience to the instructions of God.

Can you imagine what would have happened at Cana marriage if the servants had not obeyed the instructions of Mary and Jesus? Could there have been a "water turned into wine" miracle to meet their pressing needs? The resounding answer to this question is no. In the case of Naaman, could he have lived many days if he had not obeyed the voice of the man of God? I believe Naaman would have died as a leper. In either event, we can see that the overwhelming lesson is that their obedience to the word of God was the key factor to their miracles. The mighty hand of God was revealed and moved powerfully on their behalf because of their obedience. So, regardless of what your circumstances may be, your way out of all of your troubles and into victory is obedience to the word of God. There are more than eight thousand promises in the Bible and they are yours. Therefore, begin to appropriate faith and obedience and watch God, the Father, begin manifesting His word in your life. I trust that your faith has been stirred to believe God and begin to walk in your inheritance.

Chapter 15

SEVEN KEYS FOR CONTINUOUS SUCCESS

This book of the law shall not depart out of thy mouth; but thou shall meditate therein day and night, that thou mayest observe to do according to all that is written therein: for then thou shall make thy ways prosperous, and then thou shall have good success. (Joshua 1:8)

There is overwhelming evidence in the Bible to show it is the perfect "will" of God for His children to have prosperous and successful lives here on earth. In the above portion of scripture, after the death of Moses, God appointed and ordained Joshua to lead His people, the Jews. He gave him a promise to be prosperous and successful as a child of God and leader.

First, God commended Joshua to hold the book of the law in His mouth. This particular commandment, given to Joshua, was also echoed by the Apostle Paul in one of his writings: *"But what saith it? the word is nigh thee even in thy heart: that is the word of faith, which we preach" (Romans 10:8).* The Lord instructed Joshua to keep the word of the law, the Bible, in his mouth.

Secondly, God commanded him to meditate on the laws of the book, day and night. Only then, the Lord said, would He make his ways prosperous and successful. Why did God command Joshua to do this? Because the scripture says *"For with the heart man believeth unto righteousness; and with the mouth confession is made unto salvation" (Romans 10:10).*

King David also echoed the same, he wrote:

> *Blessed is the man that walketh not in the counsel of the ungodly, nor standeth in the way of sinners, nor sitteth in the seat of the scornful. But his delight is in the law of the Lord; and His law doth he mediate day and night. And he shall be like a tree planted by the rivers of water, that bringeth forth his fruit in his season; his leaf shall also not wither; and whatsoever he doeth shall prosper. (Psalms 1:1-3)*

The same commandment God gave to Joshua applies to us today. In the scriptures above, we see that God said He would make Joshua prosperous and successful. This prescription for prosperity and success still works today if we diligently adhere to the words of God. The Lord said:

> *Beloved, I wish above all things that thou mayest prosper and be in health even as thy soul prospereth.(3 John 2)*

In light of the above portions of the scriptures, let us look closely at seven keys for continuous success that the Spirit of the Lord has revealed to me. I trust that they will build up your faith and through them make you prosperous and successful. The Bible tells us:

> And the sons of the prophets said unto Elijah, Behold now, the place where we dwell with thee is too strait for us. Let us go, we pray thee, unto Jordan, and take thence every man a beam, and let us make us a place there, where we may dwell. And he answered, Go ye. And one said, be content, I pray thee, and go with thy servants. And he answered, I will go. So he went with them, and when they came to Jordan, they cut down wood. But as one was felling down a beam, the ax head fell into the water: and he cried, and said, alas, Master! For it was borrowed. And the man of God said, where fell it? And he shewed him the place. And he cut a stick, and cast it in thither; and iron did swim. Therefore said he, take it up to thee. And he put out his hand, and took it. (2 Kings 6:1-7)

YOU MUST NEVER BE CONTENT WITH WHERE YOU ARE NOW

The first key for a continuous success is that you must not be content with where you are now. Let there be no misunderstanding or confusion here! The scripture does not contradict itself. I do realize the book of Hebrews teaches:

Let your conversation be without covetousness; and be content with such things as you have: for He hath said, I will never leave thee nor forsake thee. (Hebrews 13:5)

In the context of our study I am saying that you must have a bigger vision. If you desire to be all that God has destined for you to be and have all that He has ordained for you to have and attain the height that He has set for you to reach you must never settle for less.

You must never fall into the trap of the Devil. He wants you to settle for a mediocre lifestyle. God wants His children to have and enjoy a life of abundance and greatness. So, the first key for a continued success again is that "you must never be content with where you are now." The Bible declares that:

And the sons of the prophets said unto Elisha, behold now, the place where we dwell with thee is too strait for us. (2 Kings 6:1)

The sons of the prophets were no longer content with where they were because they recognized that the place where they dwelt was too small for them to grow, multiply, and increase. They were people with foresight and recognized that anything that ceases to grow is subject to death. Without growth there is no success.

Child of God, we serve a big God and He takes delight in multiplying and increasing His children. Ironically, there are many children of God who are very little blessed in that they are content with a mediocre lifestyle. They just want to get by! If you

228

desire to be successful in all areas of your life and continue to succeed, you must never settle for anything other than your heavenly Father's very best for your life. It is God's perfect "will" that His children grow, expand, increase, and multiply to their maximum potential. The Bible tells us:

> *And God said, let us make man in our own image, after our likeness: and let them have dominion over the fish of the sea, and over the fowl of the air, and over the cattle, and over all the earth, and over every creeping thing that creepeth upon the earth. So God created man in His own image, in the image of God created he him, male and female created He them. And God blessed them, and God said unto them, be fruitful, and multiply, and replenish the earth, and subdue it: and have dominion over the fish of the air, and over the fowl of the air, and over every living thing that moveth upon the earth. (Genesis 1: 26-28)*

Right from the beginning, it has been the "will" of God for His children to multiply, increase, and enlarge.

If you are satisfied with where you are, God will not force you to grow, expand, increase, or multiply against your "will." The sons of the prophets had a desire to expand so they brought the desire to the attention of Elisha, the prophet of God. You too must have the desire to grow, expand, increase, and multiply and then bring it to the attention of your heavenly Father.

Delight thyself also in the Lord; and He shall give thee the desires of thy heart. Commit thy way unto the Lord; trust also in Him; and He shall bring it to pass. (Psalm 37:4-5)

YOU MUST PRAY FOR GOD'S GUIDANCE AND DIRECTION

The second key for a continuous success is that you must pray for God's guidance and direction. The sons of the prophets said to Elisha, the prophet of God:

Let us go, we pray thee, unto Jordan, and take thence every man a beam, and let us make us a place there, where we may dwell. And he answered, go ye. (2 Kings 6:2)

They sought approval or a signal to go from Elisha, the prophet of God, whether they should go to start a new life in Jordan or not. This step is very crucial and important because it is the foundation on which you must build if you are going to be successful in any of your undertakings. This step can be likened to the building blocks in our basement on which a big and beautiful house would rest. Without a good and solid foundation the house cannot stand. The sons of the prophet sought the face of the man of God. Even so, must we seek the face of God before we undertake any project in life. By seeking the face of God for guidance and direction we will be protected from failure and be guaranteed a successful outcome. The Bible says:

In all thy ways acknowledge Him, and
He shall direct thy paths. (Proverbs 3:6)

When the sons of the prophets sought guidance and direction from Elisha, he said, "Go ye." It is important that we seek the face of God in all the undertakings of our lives and obtain His direction, guidance, and instructions before we proceed.

YOU MUST PARTNER WITH OTHERS

The third key for a continuous success is that you must partner with others. In order to be successful in all that you do you must pray that God will bring people into your life who will contribute, help, encourage, and be in agreement with your vision and enable you to reach your desired destination. Make no mistake about this fact, you cannot be successful and maintain success without other people in your life. The sons of the prophets said unto Elisha the man of God:

Let us go, we pray thee, unto Jordan,
and take thence every man a beam.
(2 Kings 6:2)

They said to Elisha "and take thence every man a beam," everyone, not a few of them. There are always two groups of people in everyone's life. One group is people whose goal is to drag us down from reaching our potential goals. The other group is those who agree with our goals and aim to help and encourage us to reach them. We should determine which people, in our lives, are not helpful and drop them from our lives. We should strengthen our relationship with those who help us to make it. We must earnestly seek the face of the living God and pray for Him to bring us into "divine connection" with people who will help us succeed. Child of God, if you ask God for this, He will do it for you. There is no doubt that we need each other to make it, regardless of what we do.

YOU MUST BE IN PARTNERSHIP WITH GOD

The fourth key for a continuous success is that you must be in partnership with God. Regardless of your undertakings, the one sure way to guarantee success is "to never go it alone" without the living God. The surest way to guarantee failure is to "take God out of your plans." The sons of the prophets said to Elisha:

> *And one said, be content, I pray thee, and go with thy servants, and he answered, I will go. (2 Kings 6:3)*

One of the sons of the prophets, thank God for him, recognized that they would not be successful in their quest to enter Jordan without the presence and covering of the anointed man of God. Even so we must not undertake any venture without the Lord being with us. One of the sons of the prophets was wise because he knew that as long as the presence of the man of God was with them they were protected, safe and secured, blessed, and bound to have peace and success in their new location. All they needed was the presence of God. His request for Elisha's presence was granted. The man of God went with them.

YOU MUST NEVER BE ALARMED OR DISTURBED IN THE ROUGH TIMES

The fifth key for a continuous success is that you must never be alarmed or disturbed in the rough times.

There is no question whenever we operate and walk in the perfect "will" of God, the Devil fights both tooth and nail to build up opposition to us. We must never be alarmed or disturbed by this or let it stop us from getting to our desired destination. The Bible tells us that when the sons of the prophets got to Jordan and began to work, testing and difficult times arose to oppose them. They were not terribly moved because the man of God was with them.

> *But as one was falling a beam, the axe head fell into the water: and he cried, and said, alas, Master! For it was borrowed. (2 Kings 6:5)*

As we can see from the above portion of scripture, the Devil arose against the sons of the prophets and caused the head of an axe to fall into the water. In fact, this was one reason why the sons of the prophets sought the company of the man of God. They believed, "As long as God is with us, heavy storms and tornados may arise against us on our journey, but we are not alarmed knowing that greater is He who is in us than he who is against us." We must never enter the trap or temptation of jumping into ventures without the go-ahead of the living God. The Lord Jesus Christ said, *"For without me ye can do nothing."* (John 15: 5-8)

GOD WILL TURN YOUR TROUBLE INTO TRIUMPH IF YOU PARTNER WITH HIM

The sixth key for a continuous success is that God will turn your trouble into triumph if you partner with Him. Life is not perfect. As we journey, especially as we walk in the perfect "will" of God, there will be times of testing. Difficult times arise to oppose our resolve. Even so, we can count on the living God to be with us all the way to victory. One of the sons of the prophets, full of the Spirit of wisdom, requested that Elisha go with them to a new place of residence because he knew that in his companionship they would be safe. The most important thing we need to be successful and remain successful, is the presence of the living God. Elisha's presence was a shield and safekeeper for the sons of the prophets. When difficult times arose, the presence of the man of God got them covered.

> *And the man of God said, where fell it? and he shew him the place. And he cut down a stick, and cast it thither; and the iron did swim. (2 Kings 6:6)*

Child of God, this spectacular miracle happened when the axe head fell into the water. The man of God stepped in to restore it and fulfill the promise. I can't emphasize this point enough, you must not engage in any undertaking without the approval of the living God. You must partner with God to ensure success and stay successful in life.

> *Now therefore, I pray thee, if I have found grace in thy sight, shew now me thy way, that I may know thee, that I may find grace in thy sight: and*

234

consider that this nation is thy people.
And He said my presence shall go with
thee, and I will give thee rest. And he
said unto Him, if thy presence go not
with me, carry us not up hence.
(Exodus 33:13-15)

As Moses and the children of Israel journeyed through the terrible wilderness from Egypt to the promised land of Canaan, Moses prayed earnestly for God to travel and abide with them. He knew that this was the only way to ensure a successful journey to the new land. Moses even prayed that if God would not go with them that He should not allow them to go further from where they were. Moses realized that all they needed was the presence of God. We must do the same in life. We must never undertake any venture, in our lives, without God's approval and go-ahead signal.   If the Lord is with you when problems arise, you can count on Him to rescue and deliver you. The Bible tells us,

God is our refuge and strength, a very
present help in trouble. (Psalm 46:1)

YOU MUST BE PREPARED
TO DO HARD AND TEDIOUS WORK

The seventh key for a continuous success is that you must be prepared to do some hard and tedious work. As we see, the sons of the prophets were prepared to work hard building their new place of residence.

For we are laborers together with God:
ye are God's husbandry, ye are God's
building. (1 Corinthian 3:9)

235

And on the seventh day God ended his work which He had made; and He rested on the seventh day from all His work which He gad made.(Genesis 2:2)
Six days shall thou labor, and do all thy work. (Exodus 20:9)

These portions of scripture support the fact that the children of God must be a hard working group of people. We are co-laborers with the Lord Jesus Christ. The Bible records that God created the heaven and earth for six days and on the seventh day rested from His hard work. We must follow the example of our heavenly Father, the Lord Jesus Christ, and the disciples.

Ironically, many children of God want God to do it all for them. The Bible records that when Elisha, the man of God, performed a miracle by making the iron swim to shore, he commanded the son of the prophets who had lost the axe head to pick it up.

Therefore said he, take it up to thee. And he put out his hand, and took it (2 Kings 6:7)

In another words, Elisha commanded the man, "Do your part." God will assuredly do and perform those things that we cannot do if we do what is within our capability. We are co-laborer with the Lord.

Child of God, these keys for continuous success can be summed up in these few words "In all that you do, be sure to get God involved." It is very crucial that we partner with God in ventures we undertake because if we are in partnership with God, success and victory are guaranteed. When troubles arise, our hearts are not moved. So let's organize our ventures and undertakings and get our heavenly Father involved!

Chapter 16

WHY FOLLOW JESUS?

And in the morning, rising up a great while before day, he went out, and departed into a solitary place, and there prayed. And Simon and they that were with him followed after him. And when they had found him, they said unto him, all men seek for thee. (Mark 1:35-37)

The Bible tells us that when our Lord, Jesus Christ started His earthly ministry, His fame spread beyond the region. This was because of the unusual authority with which He taught people the incorruptible word of God and because of miracles He performed among the sick, diseased, and oppressed folk. As a result of the unusual happenings around the Lord's earthly ministry, the Bible records that great multitudes began to follow Him wherever He went. But were these great multitudes of people following Him for the right reasons? Are many of us today following the Lord, like those great multitudes during the Lord's earth ministry? The scripture further tells us that the motives of those following after the Lord were exposed when the Lord taught the people regarding the deeper things of God.

Many therefore of his disciples, when they had heard this, said, this is a hard saying; who can hear it? When Jesus knew in Himself; that His disciples murmured at it, He said unto them, doth this offend you? From that time many of his disciples went back, and walked no more with Him. Then said Jesus unto the twelve, will ye also go away? Then Simon Peter answered him, Lord, to whom shall we go? Thou hast the words of eternal life. And we believe and are sure that thou art that Christ, the Son of the living God.
(John 6:60-61, 66-69)

As I pointed out earlier, it is very obvious that people followed Him everywhere He went because He was doing good things for them. *"God anointed Jesus of Nazareth with the Holy Ghost and with power. He went about doing good and healing all that were oppressed of the Devil for God was with Him" (Acts 10:39).* The question that many scholars have asked and tried to answer for hundred of years is this: "Why were those great multitudes of people following after Him?" Were they following Him because He was the Son of God and they loved His teaching and preaching? What were the motivating factors that made them throng to the Lord? Let us explore this question for faith building, exhortation, edification, and spiritual enrichment.

We find, from the portion of scripture above, that the motives of those that followed were wrong motives.

And there was in their Synagogue a man with an unclean spirit; and he cried

238

out, saying, let us alone, what have we to do with thee, thou Jesus of Nazareth? Art thou come to destroy us? I know thee who thou art, the Holy One of God. And Jesus rebuked him, saying, hold thy peace, and come out of him. And when the unclean spirit had torn him, and cried with a loud voice, he came out of him. And they were all amazed, inasmuch that they questioned among themselves, saying, What thing is this? What new doctrine is this? For with authority commandeth he even the unclean spirits, and they obey Him. And immediately His fame spread abroad throughout all the region round about Galilee. (Mark 1:23-28)

Child of God, we see that the people did follow and throng after the Lord for wrong reasons. They followed Him because He was miraculously healing and feeding them. They were not following Him because of the words of God that he taught.

Dear friend, why are you following Jesus Christ today? It is very important that we settle this critical question once for all. Failure to resolve this question may bring frustration into our walk and relationship with the Lord. To assist us to resolve this critical question let us investigate the characteristics of those who know why they are following Jesus Christ.

A PERSONAL WALK AND RELATIONSHIP WITH THE LORD NOT A RELIGIOUS RELATIONSHIP

First, those who know why they are following the Jesus Christ have a personal walk and relationship

239

with the Lord and not a religious relationship/

How can one follow a person he or she does not know? In order for us to follow the Lord, we must have a personal relationship with Him and not a religious relationship. As we saw and discussed earlier, many people thronged and followed after the Lord without having a concrete, personal relationship with Him. In other words, most of the people followed without experiencing the new birth. The Bible says,

> There was a man of the Pharisees named Nicodemus, a ruler of the Jews. The same came to Jesus by night, and said unto Him, Rabbi, we know that thou art a teacher came from God: for no man can do these miracles that thou doest, except God be with Him. Jesus answered and said unto him, verily verily, I say unto thee, except a man be born again, he cannot see the kingdom of God. Nicodemus saith unto Him, how can a man be born when he is old? Can he enter the second time into his mother's womb, and be born? Jesus answered, verily, verily, I say unto thee, except a man be born of water and of the Spirit, he cannot enter into the Kingdom of God. That which is born of the flesh is flesh, and that which is born of the Spirit is Spirit. Marvel not that I said unto thee, ye must be born again. (John 3:1-7)

Friend, this statement made by the Lord was not a suggestion but a command! He said, "ye must be born again." In order for us to be true followers of the Lord Jesus Christ, we must be "born of the Spirit and of Water." To have a personal relationship with the Lord and be a true follower of the Lord means that

- First, we must acknowledge our sins and confess them to the Lord and ask for forgiveness.
- Second, we must receive the Lord into our hearts as our personal Lord and Savior.
- Third, we must commit wholeheartedly to follow the Lord as long as we live, come what may.
- Fourth, we must make a public identification, declaration, and confession of His lordship over our lives.

These four salvation steps bring you and the Lord Jesus Christ into union, relationship, and fellowship. The great multitude we discussed above, following the Lord throughout His earthly ministry, had no personal walk and relationship whatsoever with the Lord Jesus Christ. Hence they never realized why they were following the Master.

Child of God, if I may ask, why are you following Jesus Christ? In other words, why are you a Christian? Indeed, those who know why they are following Jesus must have a personal walk and relationship with Him and not a religious relationship.

When we receive and commit our lives to the Lord the promises of God become our portion. *"But as many as received Him, to them give he the power to become the sons of God, even to them that believe on His name" (John 1:12).*

FOLLOW HIM DAILY NOT SEASONALLY

Secondly, those who know why they are following the Lord Jesus Christ follow him daily. The great multitude of people that followed our Lord during His earthly ministry were seasonal and not committed followers of the Lord. They were uncommitted folk who came and followed after the Lord not necessarily because they loved what He was teaching the people but because they wanted their needs met by the miraculous hands of the Master. They that know why they are following the Lord must commit themselves to follow Him daily.

The Bible tells us

> And He said to them all, if any man will come after me, let him deny himself, and take up his cross daily, and follow. For whosoever will save his life shall lose it: but whosoever will lose his life for my sake, the same shall find it. For what is a man advantaged, if he gain the whole world, and lose himself, or be cast away. For whosoever shall be ashamed of me and my words, of him shall the Son of Man be ashamed, when He shall come in His glory, and in His father's, and of His holy angels. (Luke 9:23-26).

Child of God, there is overwhelming evidence in the Bible to support the fact that those who know why they are following Jesus Christ strive to follow Him daily and not seasonally. The Apostle Paul is a very good example of a committed person who pursued and followed after the Lord Jesus Christ daily. In one of his writings, he wrote *"I protest by your rejoicing which I have in Christ Jesus our Lord, I die daily"* (1 Corinthians 15:31).

BE NOT ASHAMED TO CONFESS JESUS CHRIST BEFORE OTHER PEOPLE

Thirdly, those who know why they are following after the Lord Jesus Christ are not ashamed to confess Him before others.

One of the striking observations regarding the great multitude of people who followed the Lord was that they never acknowledged His Lordship. They never identified with the Lord nor confessed Him publicly as their Lord and Savior. Maybe they were afraid of the rulers of their time or afraid of persecution and backlash if they openly embraced the gospel of the Lord. Whatever reasons they may have had, there is no question today there are as many hidden disciples or followers of Jesus Christ as in the days of our Lord's earthly ministry. Those who know why they are following Jesus Christ must confess Him openly as the Lord and Savior of their lives. By identifying openly with the Lord, before others, we declare to the world our decision to follow the Lord, come what may. In one of the Apostle Paul's letters he boldly wrote *"For I am not ashamed of the gospel of Christ: for it is the power of God unto salvation to every one that believeth: to the Jew first and also to the Greek" (Romans 1:16).*

Paul was not ashamed of the gospel of Christ because he was a committed follower of the Lord Jesus Christ. He boldly confessed Him openly before other people. We must all come out of our closets and openly acknowledge the living God's Son as our Lord and Savior. In addition, the Lord emphatically said *"Whosoever therefore shall confess me before men, him will I confess also before my Father which is in heaven, but whosoever shall deny me before men, him will I also deny before my Father which is in heaven" (Matthew 10:32-33).* We, as children of the living God, must never be afraid to openly identify ourselves with our Lord and

Savior, Jesus Christ and to boldly confess and follow the Lord regardless of persecution and even death, for the sake of the Lord and the gospel.

NEVER GO BACK WHEN THE GOING GETS TOUGH BUT ENDURE HARDSHIP AS A GOOD SOLDIER

Fourthly, those who know why they are following after the Lord Jesus: are committed to the cause of the Kingdom of God. They never abandon their post and retreat when the going gets rough and tough. As good soldiers of the cross of our Lord Jesus Christ we must be very determined never to turn back after we have tasted the goodness of the Kingdom of God, regardless of the challenges life brings our way. Those who don't know why they are following the Lord run away immediately when they encounter opposition. The Apostle John wrote of an event that took place after one of the Lord's teachings. He recorded

> *Many therefore of His disciples, when they had heard this said, this is a hard saying, who can hear it? When Jesus knew in Himself that His disciple murmured at it, he said unto them, doth this offend? From that time many of disciples turned back, and walked no more with Him. Then said Jesus unto the twelve, "Will ye also go away?" Then Simon Peter answered Him, Lord, to whom shall we go? Thou hast the words of eternal life; and we believe and are sure that thou art that, the Son of the living God. (John 6:60-61, 66 69)*

244

In this portion of scripture, we see that many followers deserted Him because His teachings were not what they had expected and confirmed that they did not know why they were following the Lord in the first place. They deserted the Lord Jesus Christ because they were uncommitted followers of the Lord.

Child of God, note that after the uncommitted disciples left the Lord, the Lord turned to the remaining disciples and said unto them "Will ye also go away?" Simon Peter answered Him, saying. Lord, "To whom shall we go? Thou hast the words of eternal life. And we believe and are sure that thou art that, the Son of the living God." We see the emphatic response of Simon Peter because he "believed and was sure" of the twelve's resolve and commitment to the Lord.

We are soldiers of the cross of the Lord Jesus Christ. As good soldiers we must train ourselves to endure hardship. The Apostle Paul also charged us to do the same. He wrote *"This charge I commit unto thee, son Timothy, according to the prophesies which went before on thee, that thou by them mightest wage a good warfare" (1Timothy 1:18).* And *"Thou therefore endure hardness, as a good soldier of Jesus Christ."*

Remember that our Lord never promised us a battle-free life, but, He guaranteed us a defeat-free life. Job wrote, *" Man that is born of woman hath but a few days and full of troubles" (Job 14:1).* That we are committed followers of the Lord does not exempt us from the battles of life. In fact, it signals the beginning of battles against the kingdom of darkness. The scripture tells **us**, in one of the writings of King David, *"Many are the afflictions of the righteous but the Lord delivereth him from them all. He keepeth his bones and none of them is broken" (Psalms 34:19-20).*

Child of God, our commitment to follow the Lord Jesus Christ should be solid regardless of the challenges of life's journey. Life is not perfect because of our old sinful nature. As we follow the Lord Jesus Christ, our victory key is that we keep our eyes on Him, regardless of the troubles, warfare, and challenges that cross our path. We continue knowing very well that without the cross there is no crown. The scripture exhorts us with these encouraging words:

> Looking unto Jesus the author and finisher of our faith: who for the joy that was set before him endured the cross, despising the shame, and is set down at right hand of the throne of God. For consider Him that endured such contradiction of sinners against Himself, lest ye be wearied and faint in your minds. (Hebrews 12:1-2).

HAVE THIS HOPE

Finally, those who know why they are following the Lord Jesus Christ must have a great and immovable hope of His appearing. The Lord told us before He ascended into heaven.

> Let not your heart be trouble: ye believe in God, believe also in me. In my Father's house are many mansions: if it were not so, I would have told you. I go to prepare a place for you. And if I go to prepare a place for you, I will come again, and receive you into myself: that where I am, there ye may be also. (John 14:1-3).

Those who know why they are following the Lord Jesus Christ have this unwavering and immovable hope of our Lord's appearing. Jesus Christ is coming again! Are you ready to meet with Him?

The Apostle Paul exhorts us with the words of God to patiently wait for His appearing and the rewards that He brings when He appears again. He wrote *"When Christ, who is our life, shall appear, then ye also appear with Him in glory" (Colossians 3:4).*

Just like Paul, we must endure hardship as a good soldier of Jesus Christ and fight a "good fight of faith" knowing that our rewarder is coming soon. He wrote,

> *I have fought a good fight, I have finished my course, I have keep the faith. Henceforth there is laid up for me a crown of righteousness, which the Lord, the righteous Judge, shall give me at that day: and not to me only, but unto all them that love His appearing. (2Timothy 4:7-8).*

Child of God, this book "God's Got You Covered" is aimed towards building the faith of God that is already inside of you so you can believe God for your breakthrough today! Regardless of the mountains that you must climb, "God has got you covered!"

CHAPTER 17

WORDS OF PERSONAL WITNESS
What God Has Done for Me
He Will Do For You

Jesus said unto him, if thou canst believe, all things are possible to him that believeth (Mark 9:23)

I was born fifty years ago into the lovely family of Mr. & Mrs. Paul A. Udeh. We lived in a small farming community, the town of Obamkpa, in the Delta State of Nigeria, West Africa. My father was a farmer and my mother was a small farm crop trader. My father had two wives (this is an acceptable practice in Nigerian culture) with thirteen wonderful children. During my early childhood, life was not easy for me although my parents were financially able to take adequate care of our vital needs such as food, clothing, and shelter.

In those days, education was seen, by my parents and thousands of other parents in small farming communities, as the privilege of a handful of financially well-to-do families, not for all. Due to this attitude and other primitive notions my desire to go to school was thwarted. (I later became the first person in my immediate and extended family to attend college. But, it was not an easy task.)

In 1969, I completed my sixth grade coursework. Due to the financial challenges of my parents, they were not in a position to send and sponsor me through junior high school, at that time a very expensive choice in Nigeria. I believed then and believe now there is no question about the fact that one's ticket to a brighter and better future is through education.

As you may have already discovered, I did not have the opportunity to get highly educated. My early desire for a better education and brighter future looked very dim, based on the obstacles and hindrances in the environment in which I was raised. I never ceased to keep my dreams and hope alive for a better and brighter future.

Whenever I was down and almost hopelessly out, the Bible passages I learned at the Pilgrim Baptist Elementary School became my source of hope and strength. They were the building blocks I desperately needed to keep on moving forward and believing God for a better tomorrow. The Bible tells us:

> *Then the word of the Lord came unto me, saying, Before I formed thee in the belly I knew thee; and before thou camest forth out of the womb I sanctified thee, and I ordained thee a prophet unto the nations.*
> *(Jeremiah 1:4-5)*

It was hard for me, especially seeing some of my closest friends whose parents were financially well-to-do, leave our small farm community to continue their educational journey in the cities. Along with the financial position of my parents, another blockade for my quest to further education was that I was the second male son of my father. It is customary practice, in my community, that the first male child of the family is the heir to all that the family owns. That person is also the only person entitled to be educated. This means that the rest of the children in the family are on their own.

These obstacles made it difficult for me to make headway with the limited options I had. It was difficult to better my life and break the cycle of poverty and illiteracy in my family. Although, boxed in by every imaginable obstacle, I was very determined not to be a failure in life.

I STEPPED OUT BY FAITH

In 1970, after the Nigerian civil war I left my small farm community. I went to Lagos the industrial capital of Nigeria, about four hundred miles away, to seek unskilled labor employment. This was an uphill venture because my chances of securing unskilled employment was slim. There were many more qualified candidates seeking the same employment.

But, I was as bold as a lion and very determined to change the course of my life! I was tired of living a wishful life style! I was very determined to make it, regardless of challenges and blockades in my path.

When I got to Lagos, in the month of April of that year, I resided with one of my aunties. As anticipated, things were very rough for me. Horrible opposition rose up against me everywhere I turned. Nothing seemed to work for me. It was a very difficult period of my life.

At a certain point, I was no longer able to bear the day after day pressure. I gathered my handful of belongings and headed home. It was one of the most unforgettably heartbreaking disappointments of my entire life. I remember very well that I was badly depressed and heartbroken for weeks as a result of what I called an "adventure that went wrong." I lamented for weeks because I believed that life had dealt me a big blow that knocked me out cold but did not crush me. In spite of the setbacks, my spirit refused to lie down and lick the wounds. I said to myself, with tears running down my cheeks as I departed Lagos on a blue sky, breezy cool morning, "I shall return." I took a deep breath and began to encourage my poor, broken soul with words such as "Though I am down it doesn't mean that I am out."

I WILL RETURN

I stayed in my hometown for seven hard and difficult months. In December of the same year, I went back to Lagos to continue the journey I had started several months earlier. I was still seeking an unskilled job, but this time, I was very determined to make it no matter what I had to endure.

One cool and breezy afternoon, everything was very calm and I was left alone at my aunty's home. As I looked for something to do my eyes fastened onto a little booklet in the adjacent corner of the room from where I was sitting. I hastily picked up the booklet and discovered, amazingly enough, it was a little prayer book. I began to read through the pages. The more I read the prayers the more I felt strength, hope, faith, and confidence building up inside of my heart and whole being. The little prayer booklet became the source of inspiration I desperately needed to keep my quest for employment going. In fact, I finished reading through the entire little prayer booklet in a short period of time. The booklet became my source of faith and constant companion. I read and reread the prayers in the book. I would read and pray before I left home, in the morning, to seek employment. I read again when I returned. In time, I almost memorized the entire little prayer booklet. It was a God-sent helper to me.

THE LORD GUIDED ME TO MY BREAKTHROUGH

And thine ears shall hear a word behind thee, saying, this is the way, walk ye in it, when ye turn to the right hand, and when ye turn to the left. (Isaiah 30:21)
In all thy ways acknowledge Him, and He shall direct thy paths. (Proverbs 3:6)

As I persevered, seeking the face of God concerning my situation, my faith and hope grew stronger and stronger that the power of the living God would help me secure employment. I could feel the Lord's guidance, on a daily basis, leading and directing my footsteps. As I sought the face of God fervently, He brought people into my life to help me.

In the month of January 1971, my breakthrough finally came! Oh what a glorious unforgettable day it was! I was hired by the Union Trading Company (UTC) Nigerian Limited. My job was as a "helper" in the Motor Painting Department of the company. It was the breakthrough I had waited for all my life. It was a new day for me and marked the beginning of great things to come in my life.

Even as I write this faith-building book, I can recall vividly how sweet and joyful it was for me that day. My employment breakthrough was so fulfilling that it wiped all the tears and sorrows from my eyes. My sense of hopelessness and failure was instantaneously healed. As a result of this marvelous breakthrough, my past miseries seemed to vanish

253

from my soul and I was overwhelmed with joy and peace. Above all, I had overpowering faith and new hope for a brighter future. The Bible says,

Weeping may endure for a night, but joy cometh in the morning (Psalm 30:5)

My employment breakthrough was a marvelous miracle from the hands of the living of God. Although the hourly wage was nothing to write home about, it meant so much to me. I cannot effectively describe, in words, the feelings that possessed my soul. Our God is great!

While I rejoiced, celebrated, and testified to God's goodness, the Devil ambushed my employment and stole the job from me. I was fired as a result of my misjudgment and foolishness. The circumstances that led to my firing were the result of my own stupidity and unprofessional behavior and not because God was unable to keep and sustain the job for me. The sin I committed was lying, and was caught. I tried to get paid for activities that I did not perform.

The job lasted for only three and half months. It was a heartbreaking loss and a very painful one! In my quest to start over I humbled myself and repented for my misdeeds. God, in his mercy, forgave me of all of my sins. The Bible tells us,

My little children, these things write I unto you that ye sin not. And if any man sin, we have an advocate with the Father, Jesus Christ the righteous. And He is the propitiation for our sins: and not for our's only, but also for the sins of the whole world. (1John 2:1-2)
If we confess our sins, He is faithful and

*just to forgive us our sins, and to
cleanse us from all unrighteousness
(1John 1:9)*

Child of God, there is no doubt about it that sin is
the root of all troubles and hinders and robs us of our
success but repentance brings us restoration!

THE GOD OF A SECOND CHANCE

*Seek ye the Lord while he may be
found, call ye upon him while he is
near. Let the wicked forsake his way,
and the unrighteous man his thoughts:
and let him return unto the Lord, and he
will have mercy upon him, and to our
God, for he will abundantly pardon.
(Isaiah 55:6-7)*

Child of God, there is no question we serve the
God of a second chance. When I foolishly lost my
miracle job, I went back to the drawing board. I went
on my knees in repentance and asked God to forgive
my wicked deeds and by faith obtained forgiveness
from God. The Bible says,

*If we confess our sins, he is faithfulness
and just to forgive us our sins, and to
cleanse us from all unrighteousness.
(1 John 1:9)*

Again, I began to seek another place of
employment with greater vigor and persistent faith
and determination. In the second week of June 1971,
merciful God gave me a second chance with another
company. It was a much better opportunity than the
first job I had.

255

This time around, I obtained employment with Mandilas Nigerian Limited, Air-Conditioning Division, as an apprentice air conditioning technician. It happened that I paid a visit to my friend at Mobil Oil Nigerian Limited. While I was there, I saw a little service card sitting on one of the window air conditioner in that office. Immediately, I jotted down the address of Mandilas Nigerian Limited. I later discovered that the company was the sole distributor of Carrier Heating & Air-Conditioning in Nigeria. A very large engineering firm!

The morning after visiting my friend I went to Mandilas to submit my application for employment. When I got there, I was directed to the Service Manager of the air-conditioning division, Mr. Allen Rodge, a Briton. He took my application and hastily read through it. Then, staring at me, he said, "Edward, I will reply to you." I left his office and went back home.

The next morning, I walked more than eighteen miles to Mandilas with a second application for Mr. Rodge. Again, he politely received the application from me and went over it. Again he gazed at me for few minutes and said with a heavy tone "Edward, I will reply to you." I quietly left his office and returned the next day with my third consecutive application for employment.

When I got there, very early in the morning, I went into his office not knowing what was going to happen to me. I wondered whether he was going to ask the security guards to throw me out of the premises. In fact, I thought of many bad things that could happen to me. But, I was very desperate and was determined to go into his office to submit my application for the third time, regardless of the consequences. This time, Mr. Rodge, with great astonishment on his face, gently took my application from my hand and again went through it. He sat back on his huge executive blue leather chair. Stretching backward he took off his sunglasses and looked speechlessly at me for about five minutes.

At this point we were kind of staring at each other. Needless to say, my legs were frozen to the floor and trembling not knowing why he was staring at me. The more he looked at me the more I became terrified, not knowing what was going through his mind. Again, he gently said to me, "Edward, I will reply to you." Sluggishly, I walked out of his office.

I went back to Mr. Rodge's office three more consecutive times with the same outcome. But, on my seventh visit, when I came into his office, I met another man who happened to be his assistant. Mr. Rodge pulled out my six previous applications and handed them over to his assistant. His assistant said to him, "Why not hire him?"

Mr. Rodge turned and said to me, "Edward, come and start work tomorrow at 8 am." Hearing that good news, I raced out of his office with overwhelming joy. The God of a second chance did it for me again!

It was a big second chance that the Lord gave me and a great one! I will be ever grateful to Him for what He has done for me. I am glad to say that through this opportunity, I was able to pay my way through the British Institute of Engineering Technology, a correspondence technical and engineering school, from which I graduated in December of 1975. I also completed the General Certification of Education, (GCE).

While still employed, I was able to obtain the Nigerian Trade Test-Class Three Certificate in Air-Conditioning. As God would have It, I was with the company for eight good years. It is amazing to say that I did not know that I was practicing the principle of "persistent faith and determination."

Not until after I converted did I discover that I was practicing and acting upon the word of the Lord in Luke 18:1-8. Praise God! Regardless of your challenge, the Lord is very much able to turn it all around and make miracles out of your messes. All you need to make your breakthrough come through is a "persistent faith and determination." You can do it also! This powerful spiritual law works regardless of circumstances. Give it a chance!

GOD MADE MY DREAMS COME THROUGH

In May 1976, the Lord Jesus Christ came into my life, redeemed my soul from everlasting destruction and wrote my name in the book of life. My new walk and relationship with the heavenly Father marked the beginning of tremendous, marvelous, and great manifestations of the living God in my life. It totally transformed and turned my whole life around for the best.

Immediately after my conversion, with the favor of God now upon my life in a new way, I was promoted to the position of a Senior Technician. Basking in my new walk and relationship with the living God, opportunities began to unfold in my life like I had never experienced before. Three years after my conversion, the Lord blessed me with a precious and God-fearing young lady to be my wife. On March 25, 1979, my wife and I got married. He has favorably blessed us with seven wonderful children. To God be all the Glory for great things He has done!

However my quest and dreams to further my education and brighten my chances for a better future was still burned in my bones. In 1983, my dream came through when the Lord opened the door for me to study overseas.

As the Lord would have it, today I am a proud holder of a Bachelor of Science in Electrical Engineering, University of Minnesota, and in my final year studying for the MBA at Metropolitan State University in St. Paul, MN. My dream to become the first person in my family to attend a higher institution of learning was realized because of the marvelous gifts of the living God. I will ever be grateful!

Child of God, I share my testimony to build up your faith to believe God for what may seem to be your impossibility. Regardless of what your dreams may be, I want to encourage you to never let go because God is able to make it happen. You must never forget that as you pursue your dreams, you are going to encounter some opposition, challenges, and difficulties but you must never back down because God has got you covered.

WHAT GOD DID FOR ME HE CAN DO FOR YOU

> *Then Peter opened his mouth, and said, of a truth I perceive that God is no respecter of persons. (Acts 10:34)*

The Lord wants to bless you and help you realize your dreams. Regardless of your heart desire, the Lord Jesus Christ wants to help you attain it. He has all the power to help you succeed in life because that is His good "will" and pleasure for you. Our heavenly Father said:

> *Behold, I am the Lord, the God of all flesh: is there any thing that is too hard for me? (Jeremiah 32:27)*
> *What shall we then say to these things? If God be for us, who can be against us? He that spared not his own Son,*

259

but delivered him up for us all, how shall he not with him also freely give us all things? (Romans 8:32)

So, whatever your dream in life may be I encourage you, in the Lord, never let go. Sometimes, it may seem you are not going to make it, but fix your eyes on the Lord. The closer you are to your breakthrough the harder the Devil will fight against you so be strong and stay on course. The Devil may be telling you, even as you read through the pages of this book, that you don't have what it takes to make your dreams happen. But, these are lies from the pit of hell! He is ignoring that God has got you covered! He needs to be reminded!

The Devil is a liar and every thing he tells you are lies. You have everything it takes to attain your dreams. Because God has got you covered! The blood of our Lord Jesus Christ has already won the battles of life for you. All that you need to do is to,

Commit thy way unto the Lord; trust also in Him; and He shall bring it to pass. (Psalm 37:5)
Trust in the Lord with all thine heart; and lean not unto thine own understanding. In all thy ways acknowledge Him, and He shall direct thy paths. Be not wise in thine own eyes: fear the Lord, and depart from evil. (Proverbs 3:5-7)

Child of God, entrust your life and dreams to the caring hands of God, then watch Him perform His marvelous and tremendous good works in your life. Our Lord Jesus Christ said, "I am come that they might have life and that they might have it more abundantly" (John 10:10). He came to do you good, in all the areas of your life, not evil. Never entertain the deceptive thoughts of the Devil to give up. Your breakthrough is around the corner! You are closer to reaching your dreams than you know. You may feel things are not going well for you. That is all right, just stay with it and keep on moving forward. Every day brings you closer to your destiny in the Lord. Let me conclude with a story encouraging you to maintain hope!

In a certain town, there was a King. And the King had only one son. There was also in that town a lame young man born into one of the poorest families. It came to pass that the parents of the young lame man died. The King, out of compassion, took over responsibility for the young lame man. He brought him into his palace to care for him.

It also came to pass that the only son of the King, who ate with silver spoons and had everything in abundance began to act up and complain, sorrowfully and continuously that life was not good for him. As time went by, the only son of the King began to contemplate taking his own life.

One cool day, while everybody in the palace had gone out except for the young lame man, the King's son took a rope and went to an upper area of the house above where the young lame man was sitting. He tied the rope to one of the poles overlooking the executive dining room.

261

When the young lame man looked up and saw him tying the rope, he said to the King's son, "What are you doing?"

The King's son replied, "I am tying the rope to the pole to hang myself today, I don't want to live any longer because life was not fair to me."

The young lame man paused for few moments and said, "Please make sure you tie the rope very hard so that when you hang yourself, the rope will be strong enough to keep you from falling. If the rope is not tied hard to the pole you might land on my head and kill me. Then I will never know what my life will be tomorrow."

The King's son said to himself, "Here I am, with everything at my disposal yet I was about to kill myself. Yet this young lame man who has nothing to live for has more hope for tomorrow than I do when I have everything."

Then the King's son cut down the rope and began to be thankful for what he had in life. He joined the young lame man in looking forward to brighter and better tomorrows.

The point of the story is that we must never loose hope. Although, the young lame man was in a hopeless and undesirable physical condition he did not gave up hope in life. He kept his belief that his hopeless condition could change in the future. Child of God, never give up regardless of the challenges life throws in your path because God has got you covered. **GOD HAS GOT YOU COVERED!**